Buddhism For Beginners

Plain and Simple Guide to
Buddhist Philosophy Including
Zen Teachings, Tibetan Buddhism,
and Mindfulness Meditation

Judith Yandell

Copyright © 2019 Judith Yandell

All rights reserved.

In no way is it legal to reproduce, duplicate, or transmit any part of this document in either electronic means or in printed format. recording of this publication is strictly prohibited and any storage of this document is not allowed unless with written permission from the publisher. all rights reserved. The information provided herein is stated to be truthful and consistent, in that any liability, in terms of inattention or otherwise, by any usage or abuse of any policies, processes, or directions contained within is the solitary and utter responsibility of the recipient reader. under no circumstances will any legal responsibility or blame be held against the publisher for any reparation, damages, or monetary loss due to the information herein, either directly or indirectly. Respective authors own all copyrights not held by the publisher. The information herein is offered for informational purposes solely, and is universal as so. the presentation of the information is without contract or any type of guarantee assurance. The trademarks that are used are without any consent, and the publication of the trademark is without permission or backing by the trademark owner. all trademarks and brands within this book are for clarifying purposes only and are the owned by the owners themselves, not affiliated with this document.

TABLE OF CONTENTS

Introduction 6

Chapter 1: Origins of Buddhism 10
   The Story of Siddhartha Gautama 10
   Historical Timeline of Notable Buddhist Events 15

Chapter 2: Primary Buddhist Principles and Teachings 30
   Dharma – The Path to Perfect Enlightenment 30
   The Noble Eightfold Path 35

Chapter 3: Buddhism Numbers 3 40
   The 3 Universal Truths 40
   The 3 Jewels of Refuge 42
   The 3 Higher Trainings 44

Chapter 4: Buddhism Numbers 4 46
   The 4 Noble Truths 46
   The 4 Dharma Seals 49

Chapter 5: Buddhism Numbers 5 54
   The 5 Precepts 54
   The 5 Skandhas 58

Chapter 6: Perfections of Buddhism 62
   The 6 Perfections of Mahayana Buddhism 62
   The 10 Perfections of Theravada Buddhism 69

Chapter 7: Mindfulness Meditation 74
   Knowing the Mind 76
   Training the Mind 78
   Freeing the Mind 80
   Simple Mindfulness Meditation Technique 82

Chapter 8: Karma 86

Chapter 9: Rebirth 96

Chapter 10: Bringing Buddhism into Your Everyday Life ... 106
   Practicing Buddhism 107

Conclusion 112

Other Books by Judith Yandell 114

Introduction

Welcome to *Buddhism for Beginners*. You have come to the right place to learn the basics about Buddhism, including basic principles, karma, rebirth, and mindfulness meditation. There are many aspects of Buddhism that revolve around numbers, including 3, 4, and 5. You will gain a basic understanding of the various practices tied to each number. The numbers actually make it a bit easier to remember each principle or practice, such as the 3 universal truths and 3 higher pieces of training. The final chapter of this book will show you how to incorporate Buddhism into your everyday life, should you decide that this is the philosophy by which you want to live. Yes, we said philosophy – because that is what Buddhism is, a philosophy, a way of life.

Many people hear the word, "Buddhism," and they think it is a religion. However, a person of any religion can bring Buddhist principles into their life without giving up their religious beliefs. There is no "God" to worship if you practice Buddhism. There are not Buddhist churches on every other street corner in every town in the Bible belt of the United States. There are no potluck dinners in the fellowship hall after a sermon. Buddhism can be viewed as a religion — and under that view, Buddhism is the 4th largest religion in the world — but it is much more than that, its truth goes much deeper than a traditional religion.

Buddhism is a philosophy — it is a way of living your life following a path of spiritual development that leads you to the truth of reality. There is no one definition of Buddhism because it is a practicing philosophy that you cannot truly understand until you actually experience it. However, that does not mean that this book is useless; rather, it is a guide to give you a basic understanding of the principles, beliefs, and practices of Buddhism. This will allow you to decide for yourself if Buddhism has a place in your life. Should you choose to follow the path of the Buddha, you can expect Buddhism to change your life.

The word, "budhi," from which the word, "Buddhism," is derived, means "to awaken." That is exactly what Buddhism is — an awakening that introduces your mind and spirit to a truthfulness that most people never really experience or even acknowledge. To put it in basic terms, there is one ultimate goal of Buddhism — enlightenment. This is a state of mind where you have all of the awareness and wisdom you need to view reality for exactly what it is, allowing you to live a full, happy, and peaceful life in accordance with your enlightenment. This enlightened state of mind is known as Nirvana.

There are varied schools of Buddhism, such as Zen and Tibetan. However, the basic principles and concepts are the same as the goal of enlightenment never changing. Buddhism truly is a way of life, rather than a traditional religion. There is a long history behind Buddhism, one that tells the story of the founder of this philosophical way of life. Let's begin *Buddhism for Beginners* by learning about the history behind this enlightened way of living.

Chapter 1:
Origins of Buddhism

As with any religion or philosophical teachings, there is always a starting point, a place where the idea behind the religion or the philosophy took hold, like a seed of a tree sprouting and spreading its roots. Understanding the history behind any particular religion or philosophy is the first step towards understanding the beliefs as a whole. You need to know where the beliefs came from and why in order to fully grasp their truth. Before you can even begin to learn the basics about Buddhism, you must learn the history of this great philosophy. Buddhism was not the result of a combined meeting of minds; rather, it was the result of one man's persistent desire to know the truth.

The Story of Siddhartha Gautama

Siddhartha Gautama was born below the Himalayan foothills in approximately 567 B.C.E. into the clan of Shakya, of which his father was chief. The story says that when Siddhartha Gautama was about 12 years old, the brahmins – members of the highest Hindu class, who were priests, teachers, and overall protectors of sacred learning – gave the prophecy that Siddhartha Gautama would either be a collective ruler or a celebrated holy man. His father kept him confined with the walls of the palace, where Siddhartha Gautama grew up in luxury. He was kept within the walls of the castle to prevent him from becoming a holy man, also known as an ascetic. An ascetic one who practices self-denial to the extreme, leading a simple life while pursuing spiritual goals. This was not the life his father wanted for him, so he shielded his son from the outside world in hopes that Siddhartha Gautama would grow to be a great ruler.

Siddhartha Gautama was trained to swim and wrestle, as well as training in archery and as a swordsman. Siddhartha Gautama eventually married Yaśodharā, his cousin, and they soon had a child, a son named Rāhula. It was not uncommon for royal families to marry among themselves because no other people were considered to be their equal; they wanted to keep the royal line pure. Siddhartha Gautama's life was full and rich – in today's world, he would be one of those people who simply has everything – wealth, luxury, a wife, and a child. With all of this happiness and luxury, what possible reason was there for Siddhartha Gautama to feel unsatisfied?

There was a longing inside of Siddhartha Gautama, a need to know more, a feeling of dissatisfaction with the life surrounding him. This longing led him to explore the world outside of the palace walls. In Kapilavastu, he came across 3 things: an old man, a sick man, and a dead body being taken to the grounds for burning. Siddhartha Gautama had never seen such things before during his sheltered existence – he was not prepared; he did not understand what was happening before him. His chariot driver simplified it for him – every living being gets older, faces sickness, and eventually dies. This information caused great worry and uneasiness inside of Siddhartha Gautama.

On the way back to the palace, he saw an ascetic dressed in a robe and carrying a bowl of a sadhu, or a holy man. It was then that Siddhartha Gautama vowed to leave his life of luxury in the palace, as well as his wife and child, to find the solution to all of the suffering in the world. He never woke his wife and son up to bid them goodbye; instead, he said his goodbyes under the cover of darkness, and he disappeared into the woods. There, Siddhartha Gautama used his sword to cut his long hair and donned a simple robe – a robe of an ascetic.

When Siddhartha Gautama made this choice to leave behind his royal life for that of an ascetic, he joined an entire group of men who had also left their lives behind. All of these men, including Siddhartha Gautama, were in search of blissful deliverance from individuality and suffering from the cycle of life – birth to death. Arada Kalama was his first teacher. Arada Kalama had more than 300 disciples learning his philosophy. He taught Siddhartha Gautama to train his mind to enter a state of emptiness, of nothingness. It took great discipline to reach this level of mindful peace. However, Siddhartha Gautama knew that this was not the liberation, the deliverance, that he sought, so he left the teachings of Arada Kalama, and he moved on to Udraka Ramaputra. Here, he was taught to enter a realm of his mind through concentration, a realm that was not conscious or unconscious. But again, he was dissatisfied with what he learned because he knew it was not true liberation.

Siddhartha Gautama studied and practiced various forms of concentration, philosophies, and living a simple life void of personal comforts, money, and limited food. He practiced these teachings and austerities with 5 companions over a period of about 6 years. There were times when Siddhartha Gautama seemed to be more dead than alive, a walking, breathing skeleton because he took his practices to heart. These were times when he deprived himself of everyday necessities, such as food, to a great extreme, eating only a single grain of rice each day. He practiced these austerities because he needed to take his mind to another level, one that was not dependent on his body, a level where his mind was free and liberated from the needs of his body – a level of absolute concentration and truth.

Siddhartha Gautama, still not finding the bliss and liberation that he sought, gave up being an ascetic. His 5 companions left his side when he gave up asceticism, and Siddhartha left for a village to find more substantial food. In the village, he met a woman, Sujata, who gave him a jar of honey and some milk. Siddhartha ate the honey and drank the milk, feeling his strength and resolve return to him. He went to the Nairanjana River, bathed his body clean, and went to the Bodhi tree, an old, sacred fig tree with heart-shaped leaves. The Bodhi tree later became associated with Buddhism and known as the tree of enlightenment. Under the Bodhi tree, Siddhartha Gautama spread out a mat, and he sat cross-legged to contemplate all that he had learned.

Siddhartha Gautama had listened to so many teachers, had studied so many sacred texts, and learned so many varying philosophies and methods for achieving a state of blissful liberation. So, he sat under the Bodhi tree, still and unmoving for six days, knowing there was nowhere to turn and no one to rely on except himself. On the sixth day, so the story goes, Siddhartha Gautama opened his eyes upon the morning star. It was at this time that he reached Nirvana – total enlightenment. He knew without a doubt that whatever it was that he had been looking for, it was really <u>never truly lost</u>. In fact, anyone could find it. There was no reason to struggle and live an arduous life trying to find something that was never lost – the answers were <u>all within</u> himself and within each person.

Siddhartha Gautama was 35 years old on this sixth day under the Bodhi tree. It was at this time that he became the Buddha – the Awakened One. The Buddha was also known as the Shakyamuni, the sage, or intellectual scholar or philosopher, of the Shakyas. He is believed to have said upon awakening and reaching enlightenment:

"Wonder of wonders, this very enlightenment is the nature of all beings, and yet they are unhappy for lack of it."

The Buddha had reached a state of blissful liberation, deliverance from the reality around him, a realm of his mind that brought him the peace and happiness he sought with such determination. He relished his newfound freedom and tranquility for 7 weeks. He was not inclined to share his discovery with anyone else because he was uncertain how he would explain it. But the story tells that Brahma, the chief of the 3,000 worlds, asked the Buddha to share his path to enlightenment with others, and the Buddha agreed. For approximately 45 years, the Buddha shared his knowledge with the world, creating a Buddhist community known as Sangha. He even visited his only son once more, who wound up joining the Sangha. The Buddha eventually passed away in Kushinagar.

Historical Timeline of Notable Buddhist Events

There are, of course, many more details surrounding the history of Buddhism, as well as the story of Siddhartha Gautama. As this is just a beginner's guide to Buddhism, designed to be your starting point in your Buddhist journey, we will not go over every tiny detail. However, there are notable historical events related to Buddhism. Knowing these particular periods of time and the associated events will help you as you learn about Buddhism in your own way and on your own path. Use this timeline as a reference point in all of your Buddhist learnings.

- **6th and 5th century B.C.E.**
  - Siddhartha Gautama was born.
  - Shishunaga reaches the throne and begins the Shishunaga dynasty in place of the Magadha dynasty.

- **4th century B.C.E.**
  - Kalasoka of the Shishunaga dynasty arranges the Second Buddhist council. The Sanga, the Buddhist community and following created by

the Buddha, divides into two distinct communities: the Sthaviravadins and the Mahasanghikas.
- The Nanda Empire has a period of brief domination in Magadha over Shishunaga.
- Alexander the Great arrives in Northwest India and the kingdoms that follow influence the future development of Buddhism.
- Chandragupta Maurya defeats the Nanda dynasty and conquers the majority of northern India.

- **3rd century B.C.E.**
  - The Third Buddhist council, arranged by Ashoka, creates the *Kathavatthu*, which disputes and outright contests certain heretical theories believed by some of the Buddhist groups.
  - Ashoka sends missionaries of the Buddhist beliefs to many countries, including China and Asia, to spread the teachings of Buddhism.
  - Kharosthi script inscribed at Shahbazgarhi and Mansehra in Gandhara.
  - Indian traders reach various ports of the Arabian Peninsula, spreading the teachings of Buddhism, and Ashokan monks take Buddhism to Suvarnabhumi.
  - Theravada is introduced to Sri Lanka, who was Ashoka's son.

- **2nd century B.C.E.**
  - Pushyamitra Shunga defeats the Maurya empire, creating the Shunga empire, which began a period of persecution against Buddhism.

- Demetrius I of Bactria establishes the Indo-Greek kingdom in parts of India, and Buddhism is allowed to thrive in this kingdom.
- King Menander I of the Indo-Greek kingdom converts to Buddhism under the teachings of Nagasena.
- Han Wudi, a Chinese emperor, is the recipient of 2 golden Buddha statues.

- **1st century B.C.E.**
  - Theodorus, of the Indo-Greek kingdom, preserves relics of the Buddha.
  - The Pali Canon is written down during the reign of King Vattagamini.
  - Yuezhi visits the Chinese capital to spread Buddhist teachings.

- **1st century**
  - Liu Ying becomes the first documented support of Buddhism in China.
  - Buddhism reaches China through the teachings of two monks, Kasyapa and Dharmaraksha.
  - The Chinese found the White Horse Temple, officially establishing Buddhism in China.
  - The Fourth Buddhist council is arranged under King Kanishka of Kushana in India.

- **2nd century**
  - The Kushans create a kingdom focused on Kashgar, taking control of Yarkand and Khotan.
  - A Parthian prince and Buddhist monk, An Shigao, goes to China and translates the texts of Theravada into Chinese.
  - Indian and Asian Buddhists reach Vietnam.

- Lokaksema, a Kushan monk, goes to Loyang, and he becomes the first known translator of the Mahayana into Chinese.

- **3rd century**
  - Gandhara no longer uses the Kharosthi script
  - The Skarosthi script is still used in Khotan and Niya.
  - The earliest Chinese Buddhist manuscript dates from 296.

- **4th century**
  - The University of Nalanda supports 3-10,000 monks.
  - Sundo, a monk, was sent by Fu Jian to King Sosurim of Goguryeo, establishing the making of paper in Korea.
  - Marananta, an Indian monk, goes to Baekje to bring his teachings of Buddhism to the royal family, and the king announced that all people should believe in Buddhism and find happiness.
  - Fa Xian goes from China to India, and upon his return, he translates more Buddhist text into Chinese.

- **5th century**
  - The kingdom of Funan advocates Buddhism instead of Hinduism. The stupa at Dambulla is created.
  - Kumarajiva translates more Buddhist texts to Chinese.
  - Hui Yuan states that Buddhist monks should not have to bow to the emperor.
  - Buddhism reaches Sumatra.

- 5 Gandhara monks go to Fusang to spread the teachings of Buddhism.

- **6th century**
  - Buddhism reaches Japan through Baekje (modern-day Korea).
  - Believers of Zen Buddhism come from China to Vietnam.

- **7th century**
  - Japan obtains copies of sutras from Sui, China.
  - Jingwan starts carving sutras into stone in Fangshan, Yuzhou.
  - The reign of Songtsen Gampo of Tibet begins and ends; he is the first Tibetan king to promote Buddhism in Tibet.
  - More than 1,000 Buddhist monks reside in Palembang on the island of Sumatra, Indonesia.
  - The Hwaeom school is founded by Uisang.

- **8th century**
  - Buddhist stories are translated into Syriac and Arabic. The life of the Buddha is translated into Greek by John of Damascus, and it is circulated among Christians as the story of Barlaam and Josaphat. The story of Josaphat eventually becomes so popular that he is made a Catholic saint – even though the story is actually that of the Buddha.
  - Simsang founds Japan's Kegon tradition in the Todai-ji temple.
  - Jianzhen finally reaches Japan after 11 attempts and establishes the Japanese Ritsu school.

- Construction of the Indonesian Buddhist structure, Borobodur, begins and is completed in 830 after 50 years of labor.

- **9th century**
  - Two monks, Kukai and Saicho, travel to China from Japan. Kukai returns to Japan and founds the Japanese Shingon school, while Saicho returns to found the Japanese Tendai school.
  - Langdarma rules Tibet and denounces Buddhism.
  - Ennin goes to China for 9 years, where he reaches the Buddhist mountain of Wutaishan. He keeps a detailed journal of this time, including the history of China and the persecution of Buddhism.
  - Wuzong of the Tang Dynasty rules China, prohibiting Buddhism, and completing the Great Anti-Buddhist Persecution, which weakens the structure of Buddhism in China.
  - Dongshan Liangjie founds the Caodong school of Zen in southern China.

- **10th century**
  - The construction of a Buddhist temple begins in Myanmar.
  - A revival of Buddhism begins in Tibet.
  - The Song Dynasty of China hires Chengdu woodcarvers to carve the Buddhist canon for printing. 130,000 blocks are created.
  - A printed copy of the Buddhist canon created by the Song Dynasty reaches Korea.

- **11th century**
  - The Ly Dynasty in Vietnam supports Mahayana Buddhism.
  - Korea carves its own woodblock prints of the canon.
  - The order of Bhikkhuni, Buddhist nuns, ends because of invasions in Southeast Asia but is later revived in Sri Lanka.
  - King Anawrahta of the Pagan Kingdom converts to Theravada Buddhist beliefs.
  - The printed canon from the Khitans reaches Korea from China.
  - King Kyansittha reigns in Myanmar, and he completes the construction of the Shwezigon Pagoda, which is a shrine for Buddha relics.

- **12th century**
  - During the Song Dynasty of China, when Huizong rules, Buddhism is outlawed in favor of the Dao.
  - Pure Land Buddhism is established as an independent Japanese sect by Honen.
  - Anawrahta of Pagan sends monks to reestablish Buddhism in the island kingdom.
  - Jayavarman VII constructs the Bayon, a Buddhist structure in the Angkor temple.

- **13th century**
  - The famous Buddhist educational center in Nalanda, India is looted and burned by Muhammad bin Bakhtiya Khilji.
  - The Japanese founder of Nichiren Buddhism, Nichiren Daishonin, is born.
  - The Thai kingdom of Sukhothai is created and Theravada Buddhism is the state religion.

- Dogen Zenji establishes the Eiheiji Soto Zen Temple and Monastery.
- Theravada becomes the dominant form of Buddhism in Cambodia.
- Kublai Khan declares Buddhism the state religion of the Yuan dynasty, and he creates the Bureau of Buddhist and Tibetan Affairs.
- Ram Khamhaeng, also known as Rama the Bold, reigns over Laos, Thailand, Pegu, and parts of the Malay Peninsula.
- Ilkhanate becomes a Buddhist state.
- The Pagan empire falls because of Mongolian invasions.
- Ghazan Khan, the Mongol leader, converts to Islam, ending a long line of Buddhist leaders.

- **14th century**
  - A Persian historian records about 11 Buddhist texts.
  - Persian Buddhists try to convert Uldjaitu Khan.
  - The Japanese Mugai Nyodai becomes the first female abbess and the first ordained female Zen master.
  - Keizan Zenji establishes the Sojiji Soto Zen Temple and Monastery.
  - Gyalwa Gendun Drubpa is the first Dalai Lama of Tibet.

- **15th century**
  - Zheng He, a Chinese admiral, takes 7 journeys throughout southeast Asia, the Persian Gulf, Egypt, East Africa, and India. Buddhism is well-established in China.

- **16th century**
  - Sonam Gyatso becomes the third Dalai Lama.

- **17th century**
  - Vietnam divides, and the rulers of the south support Mahayana Buddhism.
  - The Toyotomi family rebuilds an image of Buddha at the Temple of Hokoji.
  - The Oirat Mongols convert to the Geluk school of Tibetan Buddhist teachings.
  - The first Jebtsundamba Khutughtu is born in Zanabazar, and he is the great-grandson of Abadai Khan of Khalkha.
  - The sovereignty of Tibet is donated to the fifth Dalai Lama by Guushi Khan of the Khoshuud.

- **18th century**
  - Sri Lanka reinstates the Siyan Nikaya lineage of monks from Thailand.
  - The Burmese invade Ayutthaya, Thailand, and destroy many Buddhist texts.

- **19th century**
  - The first united Vietnam is ruled by Nguyen Anh, who creates a Confucianist orthodox state to halt the influence of Buddhism. He even forbids men to go to Buddhist ceremonies.
  - Minh Mang rules Vietnam, and he also puts restrictions on Buddhism. He requires monks to carry identification documents, and he starts the persecution of Catholic missionaries.
  - King Mongkut of Thailand, who was once a monk, reforms and modernizes monkhood.

- A huge revival of Buddhism occurs in Sri Lanka following a period of persecution; Buddhism continues to flourish today.
- King Mindon of Burma creates a council to edit the Pali canon. He orders the texts to be engraved upon 729 stones set up on nearby monastery grounds.
- The first Westerners to receive the refuges and precepts, which is a ceremony performed to signify becoming a Buddhist, are Madame Blavatsky and Colonel Olcott. Blavatsky is the first Western woman to receive the refuges and precepts.
- In Shanghai, China, the Jade Buddha Temple is founded with 2 Buddha statues imported from Burma.
- U Dhammaloka is ordained in Burma as the first named, but not first known, western bhikkhu.
- The World Parliament of Religions meets in Chicago.
- Nepalese archaeologists rediscover the stone pillar of Ashoka at Lumbini.
- In Myanmar, Gordon Douglas is ordained in Theravada Buddhism.

- **20th century**
  - Charles Henry Allan Bennett leads the First Buddhist Mission to the west.
  - U Dhammaloka is tried for opposition to Christian missionaries.
  - Nyanatiloka founds the first monastery for Western Theravada monks, known as the Island Hermitage, in Sri Lanka.
  - The first Soto Zen temple in North America, the Zenshuji Soto Mission, is founded.

- In Japan, Soka Gakkai is founded.
- In Sri Lanka, the World Fellowship of Buddhists is founded.
- Asoka Weeraratna founds the German Dharmaduta Society in Sri Lanka on September 21, 1952, to help spread the teachings of Buddhism in Germany.
- U Nu organizes the Sixth Buddhist council, which is held in Rangoon, Burma. This occurs in 1954, and the council ends in time to celebrate the 2500th anniversary of the death of the Buddha.
- B. R. Ambedkar, the father of the Indian Constitution, converts to Navayana Buddhism, bringing with him more than 650,000 followers, spurring the modern Neo-Buddhist movement.
- In New York City, the Zen Studies Society is founded.
- The first Theravada Buddhist Mission from Sri Lanka to Germany occurs.
- The Berlin Buddhist Vihara is established in Berlin-Frohnau, Germany.
- Caves near the summit of Pai-tai mountain are reopened to reveal thousands of Buddhist sutras carved into stone.
- The 14th Dalai Lama flees from Tibet and establishes an exiled community in India.
- Tripitaka Master Shramana Hsuan Hua founds the Dharma Realm Buddhist Association. He also founded the City of Ten Thousand Buddhas and ordained the first 5 ordained American Buddhist monks and nuns.
- Shunryu Suzuki founds the San Francisco Zen Center.

- The Burmese government arrests more than 700 monks for disregarding government rule.
- The World Buddhist Sangha Council comes to order in Sri Lanka to try and mend differences between the Theravada and the Mahayana.
- A British woman named Freda Bedi is the first Western woman to be ordained in Tibetan Buddhism.
- The first 5 American Bhikshus and Bhikshunis are ordained in the Chinese tradition.
- Borobodur is restored by the Indonesian Archaeological Service and UNESCO.
- The first monastery for training and support for western Buddhist monks, Wat Pah Nanachat, is founded in Thailand.
- In Boulder, Colorado, the Naropa Institute is founded.
- 600 monks are arrested in Burma.
- In Barre, Massachusetts, the Insight Meditation Society is founded.
- Cambodian communists try to destroy Buddhism under the order of Pol Pot, and they are almost successful. When Vietnam invades Cambodia is 1978, almost all monks and religious teachers had been killed or exiled, while almost all temples and Buddhist libraries were destroyed.
- Heng Sure and Heng Chau, in the name of world peace, make a pilgrimage from Los Angeles to the City of Ten Thousand Buddhas in Mendocino. The pilgrimage consisted of taking 3 steps and 1 bow over the distance of more than 600 miles, and it took 2 ½ years to complete.

- The monk, La Ba, is accused of being a cannibal and a murderer in Burma.
- More monks are arrested, and monasteries closed in Burma. The violence continues through the '80s.
- More than 7,000 monks meet in Mandalay, Burma to boycott the military.
- In India, the Buddha Statue is installed, made from white granite, and later consecrated by the Dalai Lama.
- In Australia, Subhana Barzagi Roshi becomes the Diamond Sangha's first female roshi, which is a Zen teacher, in 1996.
- In India, a Bhikkhuni Order is revived through efforts made by the International Buddhist Women Association.
- The Liberation Tigers of Tamil Eelam terrorists arrange a suicide attack on a sacred Buddhist site in Sri Lanka, the Temple of the Tooth, where the Buddha's tooth is enshrined. 8 civilians die and 25 more are injured.
- The first American woman to receive transmission in the Rinzai school of Buddhism is Sherry Chayat of Brooklyn.

- **21st century**
  - The Taliban destroys 2 of the world's tallest Buddha statues in Afghanistan.
  - The first bhikkhuni in the Drikung Kagyu lineage, an American woman named Khenmo Drolma, is ordained in Taiwan.
  - The first American-born woman to achieve bhikkhuni ordination in Theravada is Ayya Sudhamma Bhikkhuni.

- The first westerner installed as an abbot in the Drikung Kagyu lineage is Khenmo Drolma. She became the abbot of the Vajra Dakini Nunnery.
- Buddhist monks win nine seats in elections in Sri Lanka.
- The First World Buddhist Forum is sponsored by the government of the People's Republic of China. The Dalai Lama did not attend.
- Texan Merle Kodo Boyd is the first African-American woman to receive Dharma transmission of Zen Buddhist beliefs.
- Myokei Caine-Barrett, born in Japan, is the first female Nichiren priest of her order in North America.
- Sherry Chayat, after a 10-year training process known as shitsugo, gains the title of roshi and the name Shinge.
- The Western Buddhist Order becomes the Triratna Buddhist Order, and the Friends of the Western Buddhist Order becomes the Triratna Buddhist Community.
- The first Tibetan Buddhist nunnery is consecrated in America.
- 4 novice nuns in California are given full bhikkhuni ordination in the Thai Theravada tradition.
- The Soto Zen Buddhist Association gives its approval to a document that honors the women ancestors of the Zen tradition, including ancestors dating back 2,500 years.
- The Institute for Buddhist Dialectical Studies in India gave the degree of geshe to Venerable Kelsang Wangmo, a German num, making her the world's first female geshe.

- Tibetan women are allowed to take the geshe exams for the first time in history.
- Nalanda University in India is established to revive the seat of ancient learnings.
- 20 Tibetan Buddhist nuns became the first women of Tibet to earn their geshe degrees.

This timeline is not meant to be all-inclusive. It is merely a tool that you can use to learn about the history of Buddhism, as well as some of the more current happenings in the world of Buddhism. Each notable event on the timeline is important in one way or another to Buddhism. The timeline shows you at a glance how Buddhism has grown and developed over the years, how it has spread all over the world, and how it has become a very accepted and widely-practiced philosophy of life.

Chapter 2:
Primary Buddhist Principles and Teachings

Clearly, Buddhism has a long and rich history throughout the world. From Siddhartha Gautama's journey to enlightenment to the worldwide acceptance of Buddhism today, there is much to learn about this way of life. In this beginner's guide, the goal is to gain a broad overview of knowledge about Buddhism. Now that you understand more about how Buddhism came to be, it is time to learn about the basic principles, teachings, and philosophies practiced in Buddhism.

Dharma – The Path to Perfect Enlightenment ✓

When the Buddha reached Nirvana, he did this by following the path of the dharma. In Buddhism, dharma refers to a sort of cosmic law and order – a way of thinking that believes there is a greater force at work than anything within us; not a divine god, but a divine force that ensures the scales are always balanced. Dharma is one of the 3 jewels of the Buddha, which we discuss later. The dharma can be thought of as the binding beliefs surrounding Buddhism – binding because when the dharma is realized and acknowledged, buddhas are created; the dharma binds the Buddhist community together under the umbrella of shared philosophies.

The dharma encompasses the entire path to perfect enlightenment, from your first moment of curiosity that leads you to explore Buddhism to the final moment when you achieve Nirvana. The Buddha said that the dharma is always here, always around us. The dharma is the foundation of our reality – it is who and what we are, it is the truth of who and what we are. Buddhists want to reach this "true nature," this "true self" that lies within. They do not want to just see it and recognize it; they want to relish in it, to live in it, and to forget any other self they might have been. Buddhists know that we have no end and no beginning – it is an eternal circle of love. Everyone – even you – can follow the dharma, for this "true self" is within you, it is just on the edge of your consciousness. You only need to tap into it.

The dharma offers protection from all of the negativity around you. Buddhists believe that the problems and suffering we experience in our daily lives stems from ignorance. To eliminate ignorance, you simply have to follow the dharma. Dharma improves your quality of life. It does not focus on external factors, such as wealth and material objects, but rather, it focuses on improving your internal perception of your quality of life. True happiness comes from within, rooted firmly in your inner peace, tranquility, and joy. Buddhism teaches you that inner peace must come first; without it, there will never be peace on the outside. Inner peace is achieved through the spiritual paths of the dharma.

It is easiest to think of the dharma simply as the truth. It is your true self, your true reality, your true perception of life, your true peace, and your true happiness. The dharma teaches you how to grow mentally and intellectually – it is an expansion of your mind and your spiritual self, an expansion that reaches a level of pure bliss and peace – Nirvana. The dharma is much more than just a belief – it is a way of living your life. In fact, Buddha's teachings instructed his students to release all beliefs and speculations that they might hold.

"The Buddha or a disciple of the Buddha [teaches] the Dhamma for the elimination of all speculative views, determinations, biases, adherences, and underlying tendencies, for the stilling of all mental constructs, for the relinquishing of all attachments, for the destruction of craving, for dispassion, for cessation, for Nirvana."
—*Middle Length Discourse 22.20*

The Buddha never took a stand on other's speculation and beliefs. He did not criticize other beliefs; rather, instead of offering some sort of judgment against other speculations and beliefs, he simply said that doing so:

"Is not beneficial, does not belong to the basics of the holy life, does not lead to disenchantment, to dispassion, to cessation, to peace, to direct knowledge, to enlightenment, to Nirvana."
—*Middle Length Discourse 63.8*

The Buddha taught the dharma as a way of life, a way to end suffering, as an actual practice that you can incorporate into your everyday life to reach Nirvana. The dharma is a way to live your life. The dharma is the practice of doing no evil and purifying your mind. There are no scriptures to memorize, no commandments to follow. Instead, the dharma focuses on the actions you take in life, the way you conduct yourself in life, and the moral principles by which you should live your life. These actions include things such as not criticizing others, not hurting others, knowing and practicing moderation, understanding solitude and how it opens your mind, and to always pursue a higher and more open state of mind. The dharma not only focuses on how you live your life through moral actions, but also expanding your mind, for without the expansion of your mind to a higher level of spiritual awareness, you will never reach Nirvana, and you will never end your suffering.

The dharma is your path to being indifferent, to being unencumbered, to simplify your life and belongings, to being modest, to being content, to being independent, to being persistent in your actions and goals, and to being completely unburdened. The dharma are the Buddha's teachings, the morals, and actions that he lived by. You, too, can live by the dharma, so you can live this same peaceful, unburdened, untroubled life of simplicity and happiness. The Buddha wanted only for people to live without arguing and fighting amongst each other. He created the dharma as a sort of roadmap for people to follow, a map that leads you to a life free from the worrying, suffering, and problems that plague your life. For with the right perception of the world around you, with an enlightened state of being, the worrying, problems, and suffering no longer matter – you find your peace.

The dharma teaches you that you must first see all of the negativity in your mind before you can let go of the negativity, and live a life of peace and happiness. You have to recognize within yourself and your own mind things such as anger, hate, greed, envy, and arrogance. Once you recognize and acknowledge all of the negativity in your mind, you are free to abandon it. You consciously leave it behind, choosing to know the dharma, to live a life of peace and happiness. Imagine the liberation, the freedom, that you can experience by leaving all of the negativity behind. This includes negative thoughts and feelings, as well as actions. Negativity has an energy all its own – it seeps into your life in all of the cracks, and it takes up residence within your mind. By learning to let go, you will no longer feel the overwhelming pressure of negativity.

The dharma is within all of us; it lies dormant within every mind, body, and soul. It is the path to Nirvana, which the Buddha defined as "the destruction of greed, hatred, and delusion." You see, each individual has the dharma inside of them, it is within their reach; they only have to see it. Each person can let go of the greed, anger, hatred, and delusion within themselves, and they can live a life of peace and harmony. Imagine what kind of world we would live in if ALL people found their dharma, letting go of all of the negativity, and living in peace and happiness? You can, too, know the dharma; it dwells within you, just out of sight and out of reach. All you have to do is see it within your mind and heart, and you will achieve Nirvana.

The Noble Eightfold Path

The Noble Eightfold Path is one of the primary teachings of the Buddha. The Noble Eightfold Path is visually represented by the Buddhist symbol of the dharma wheel. The dharma wheel is one of the oldest Buddhist symbols. It is believed that the Buddha set the wheel into motion upon the delivery of his first sermon teaching about Buddhism. The wheel is a symbol of the cosmic order of things, which we know is part of the dharma – a cosmic law and order. A wheel is always in motion, always moving; hence, it symbolizes the constant movement of the cosmic order of life.

You will remember that Buddhism is the philosophy of seeking liberation from the suffering of life. The Noble Eightfold Path is a sort of guide to show you how to end the suffering that comes with every life. Almost the entire philosophy of Buddhism draws from this path. Its very essence is found within so many of the Buddha's teachings, so many of his beliefs that he spread to his disciples, and then they spread throughout the world. The 8 practices of the Noble Eightfold Path are as follows:

1. **Right understanding** – understanding the way things really are, understanding the truth of things, knowing that every action has a consequence. This practice teaches you how to truly understand the world around you, a deep understanding that only comes with a pure and developed mind.

2. **Right thought** – knowingly giving up your material home and taking on the life of simplicity, modesty, love, and kindness, extending your thoughts of love and kindness to every living creature. This practice teaches you about releasing the bad while retaining the good. It teaches you to spread the goodness to everyone you come across in life.

3. **Right speech** – never lie, never gossip or slander another in a way that brings hatred and disharmony, never speak ill, rudely, maliciously, or abusively of another person. This practice teaches you to use kind, gentle, friendly, and useful words, words that have meaning, words that have the truth. If you cannot say something useful, keep a "noble silence."

4. **Right action** – never kill or injure another, never steal, give up material things, give up illegitimate sexual acts. This practice teaches you to conduct yourself in a moral, peaceful manner, with honor. It also teaches you to lead by example, to show others how to conduct themselves in the same honorable manner.

5. **Right livelihood** – only have just enough to live, to sustain a living, never work in a trade that harm's another living creature. This practice teaches you how to live with just enough so that you made abandon greed and envy. It also reinforces war and other professions that bring with them evil and harm to others.

6. **Right effort** – letting go of the negative, embracing the positive, ridding yourself and others of evil, creating positive, good, and wholesome states of the mind. This practice teaches you to, essentially, let go of the bad while holding on to the good. It also encourages you to show others how to eliminate evil from their lives.

7. **Right mindfulness** – always mindful of the Buddhist teachings, always conscious of your actions, always aware of your feelings, your thoughts, and your ideas. This practice teaches you to always know what is going on within yourself, as well as to give careful thought to your actions. This goes hand-in-hand with letting go of the negativity and embracing the good in life. It teaches you to be always conscious and aware at every moment so that you will always put forth kindness, love, and happiness.

8. **Right concentration** – practice meditation, develop your mindfulness, train and discipline your mind. This practice teaches you the stages of meditation. This first stage is when you discard all unwholesome thoughts from your mind, feeling only joy. The second stage is when you, essentially, clear your mind of any mental activities, teaching it to become still and tranquil, while you still feel the happiness and joy. The third stage teaches you to let go of the joy while still remaining happy. The fourth stage of meditation is when you release even the feelings of happiness, when your mind is a pure place, feeling and thinking nothing, only being aware.

There is no right or wrong numerical order in which to follow the practices of the Noble Eightfold Path. The list is just that — a list of the practices. The primary goal of a burgeoning Buddhist is to develop each practice at the same time. Each practice builds upon other practices. As a Buddhist, you must work to develop the practices within yourself as far as you are capable of doing. Each practice is going to take time to nurture and develop. Do not expect immediate results — the path of Buddhism is a long one, one that is full of many, many steps.

The Eightfold Path is a path that is followed, practiced, and developed within yourself. Your path is not going to be the same as your fellow Buddhist's path. Each path is individual, each practice developed at your own pace, within your own skills. The Eightfold Path teaches you self-discipline, self-development, and self-purification. It is not a religious path upon which you will participate in a ceremony or a form of prayer or worship. This is the path of the Buddha, the very one that he followed, to reach freedom, peace, and perfect happiness — to reach Nirvana.

Chapter 3:
Buddhism Numbers 3

Throughout your journey down the path of Buddhism, you will often come across numbers. The Buddha created these numbered lists to make it easier for his followers to learn and practice Buddhism. Rather than try to learn everything all at once, you can break it up into smaller pieces, so you can focus on a particular section until you have a full understanding, until you grasp each section's truth. In these next chapters, we will focus on some of these numbered lists, these "pieces" of Buddhist teachings, that are an essential part of the core of Buddhism. This chapter brings to light number 3.

The 3 Universal Truths

The 3 Universal Truths of Buddhism are Impermanence, No Self, and Suffering. These universal truths are meant to help us understand not only ourselves and other people, but the entire world around us, the entire universe. It is believed that the Buddha discovered these truths while he was meditating outside. He looked around at the world around him, and he was confronted by the circle of life. There was so much beauty everywhere, but there was also so much suffering. Some flowers bloomed in glory, while other flowers withered up and died. He watched a bird eat a worm, and then an eagle ate that very same bird. The Buddha did not understand why life turned into death. He did not understand why some creatures had to kill others to live. He meditated, and this is when he discovered the 3 Universal Truths.

Impermanence is the knowledge of the change. Everything changes. Nothing stays the same. Just as every season changes into another, every season of your life turns into another. You are born, you grow, you marry and settle down, you have a family, you get old, and eventually, you die. The only thing that is certain in life is death. Impermanence teaches you to let go of life. You cannot cling to something that will inevitably disappear. Change is permanent – everything else is not. You must let go of every aspect of life, even those things that bring you joy because you will never be able to keep them forever. You must remember that even though death is coming for you, with death comes peace – peace from sadness and suffering. The circle of life will always go on.

No self is the knowledge that you must be selfless to attain enlightenment. The Buddha did not believe in a soul. His teachings reflected that belief. He believed in rebirth, that you have a "self" that is eventually reborn. No self teaches you to remain without ego, to live without selfishness, to renounce the "I" in your life. This means that you embrace of life without longings and desires, without wanting to own things. You must rid yourself of every want and desire to attain a level of selflessness that will lead you to

Nirvana. There is no longer an "I," there is only enlightenment, peace, and happiness. This is all you need from the world.

Suffering is at the very core of Buddhism. The Buddha teaches that suffering is a central part of our lives, of our world. Because nothing is forever, because things will always change, happiness will eventually lead to suffering. Suffering touches every aspect of your life. By following the Eightfold Path, by relinquishing all desires, you can avoid the suffering, and you can lead a life of wisdom, enlightenment, and compassion. You can help others to find relief from their suffering, too. Desire leads to suffering. We want things, from material things to necessary things, such as food and shelter. But once we get what we want, we always want more, something better. Desire creates a need for more, a need for dissatisfaction, and a need for power. Desire is at the root of suffering, so you must eliminate your desires, you must let them go, to find true peace and enlightenment.

The 3 Jewels of Refuge

Also known as the 3 Refuges or the Triple Gem, the 3 Jewels are where Buddhists can take refuge. Taking refuge in Buddhism means to seek shelter and security, a sense of safety and well-being, by taking a vow, a vow pertaining to each of the 3 Jewels. It is an intellectual and spiritual commitment to the path of Buddhism. The 3 Jewels are different levels of an awakened mind. The 3 Jewels are the Buddha, the Dharma, and the Sangha.

Taking refuge in the Buddha refers to the actual Buddha and the teachings of the Buddha. With this Jewel, you are acknowledging the Buddha as an enlightened man, not a god, who followed a specific path to Nirvana – a path that you, too, can follow. You acknowledge that the Buddha held supreme wisdom and compassion, that he was entirely pure, and that he can show you the way to enlightenment. You are also acknowledging the teachings of the Buddha. Since the actual Buddha is no longer in this world, you embrace all of the other Buddhist teachers who continue to spread his supreme knowledge around the world. You seek refuge in enlightenment, in knowing that there is a path to enlightenment, and you can follow that path to Nirvana.

To take refuge in the Dharma means to embrace the teachings of the Buddha, to know they are the truth, and to practice Buddhism with faith and trust in yourself. You must trust and accept the Dharma to practice Buddhism; you must also trust in yourself that you are mindful of the moment in practicing Buddhism. You are embracing the way to Nirvana by embracing the lessons of the Dharma. The Dharma is your guide; therefore, you seek refuge in the Dharma to protect you and to show you the way to Nirvana.

To take refuge in the Sangha is to seek support, comfort, and help from the Buddhist community. You cannot achieve enlightenment alone – you need the help of other Buddhists to assist you in finding your way to Nirvana. You can compare it to belonging to a church. When you are a member of a church, you attend that church faithfully. You actively participate in the church and its functions. You do not attend other churches of other religions because the church you attend is your church – it is your chosen religion. The Sangha is the community with which you surround yourself. Your fellow Buddhists will help you see your truth, and you will help them see their truth, as well. There are no demands in the Sangha, no expectations – it is a community of like minded people who seek enlightenment, just like you. There is a fulfillment that comes from the Sangha because you are accepted and welcomed without question and without judgment.

The 3 Higher Trainings

The 3 Higher Trainings are some of the most important aspects in the teachings of the Buddha. These trainings are essential on the path to liberation and enlightenment. Regardless of which Buddhist path you are on, which teachings you follow (Mahayana, Theravada, and Vajrayana), these 3 trainings do not change – they are essential to all the Buddhist paths. These higher trainings all work together to help you reach a state of enlightenment. The 3 Higher Trainings are ethical discipline, concentration, and wisdom.

Ethical discipline gets your mind ready for meditation. You need a clear mind to meditate. You cannot have any negativity in your mind, or you will not be able to properly meditate. You must be disciplined to simplify your life, and simple life is the way of the Buddhist. You have to make an environment around you that will help you maintain a peaceful, happy state of mind.

Concentration is that actual act of meditation. This is when you transform your mind. Through the levels of meditation, your mind becomes a clear space, free of negativity, pure and ready for enlightenment. After meditation, when your mind reaches the purest level, wisdom follows. With wisdom, you can find even more ways to simplify your life, to be disciplined. The more you discipline yourself and your life, the more you can open your mind to higher levels of meditation, which create even more wisdom. A simple, disciplined life leaves you more time and energy to devote to meditation, which leads to gaining more knowledge and awareness, which leads to more discipline.

It is easy to see that the 3 Higher Trainings are a circle of trainings that are individual and, yet, dependent on each other. Each training takes you to another level of the next, and then the circle starts over. With each time you simplify, meditate, and gain wisdom, you are that much closer to reaching enlightenment – to reaching Nirvana.

Chapter 4:
Buddhism Numbers 4

The next important number associated with Buddhism is the number 4. There are several important teachings that fall under the number 4. While there are more than just what this book covers in this particular chapter, you will have a good sense of what some of the more important teachings are after reading this chapter. As this is a beginner's guide to the world of Buddhism, a general understanding of the overall teachings and notable principles will help you on your own journey to enlightenment.

The 4 Noble Truths

The 4 Noble Truths form the basic foundation of Buddhism. They are noble because they set us free from suffering. These truths did not come into being right away; rather, they were recognized as being essential to Buddhism as the Buddha's teachings grew and spread. These truths are thought to be the Buddha's first formal teachings. The truths are the teachings Buddha gave after he reached his complete awakening after he became enlightened. These truths reflect the Buddha's experience of finally understanding the cause of and the healing of suffering. There are, of course, different stories around the truths, but the core meanings are the same, regardless of the Buddhist path. The 4 Noble Truths are suffering, the cause of suffering, the end of suffering, and the path.

Suffering is the truth that teaches you that suffering exists in everything. In all parts of your life, even the good ones, even the best memories, there is still suffering to be found. The suffering can be as traumatic as the loss of a loved one or as simple as feeling a bit of anxiety or worry or even just insecurity. Suffering comes in many different forms, and it has many different levels – however, it is all still suffering. Knowing that suffering exists everywhere, and it is a part of everything, will help you learn how to let go of the suffering. Life is never easy. However, it does not have to be full of different levels of suffering. You only need to accept that suffering exists, learn how to recognize it, and learn how to release it from your mind and your life.

The cause of suffering is the truth that teaches you where the suffering comes from – from within your mind because your mind is struggling to cope with a particular challenge. If you have suffered the loss of a loved one, your mind is full of grief and pain because it does not know another way with which to deal with the loss. If you are having financial struggles, your mind is full of anxiety because you have responsibilities to fulfill. However, if you let go of the idea that you are independent of the universe, that you are an "I" when you must release the "self," you will find the suffering decreases. The cause of suffering is a product of your mind and your arrogance and your ignorance. When you accept your part in causing your own suffering, you will be able to end the suffering.

The end of suffering is the truth that teaches you that, even though life is full of suffering, and you contribute to your own suffering, there is still the possibility of a life without suffering. There are things standing in the way of your peace and happiness. However, there is always an end to the suffering in sight. You are not destined to live a life of suffering. You need only to follow the right path to learn how to let go of the things that bring you suffering. When you reach enlightenment, when you attain Nirvana, your mind will be pure. You will be awakened, just like the Buddha, and you will no longer suffer.

The path is the truth that teaches you the Eightfold Path, which is the path to enlightenment. By following the Eightfold Path, by living your life by the teachings of the Buddha, you will reach enlightenment. You will reach Nirvana. You will wake up, just as the Buddha did, and you will hold the key to your own peace and happiness – not in your hand, but within yourself. Through ethical living, meditation, and gaining wisdom, you will find your happiness.

The underlying message of the 4 Noble Truths is simple – you must be aware, you must pay attention, and you must see the truth clearly to live a life of love and joy, and to spread this love and joy to everyone around you. That is the basic premise of Buddhism – a life of peace, love, and happiness. It sounds easy enough when you read it, but to actually accomplish enlightenment, to actually reach Nirvana, requires much more than just reading a few words or saying a few vows. Buddhism is a lifestyle. It is the way you will live your life each and every day. It is the way you will treat others in your life, even if they treat you poorly. Buddhism is being awoke; it is knowing the truth; it is understanding; it is awareness; it is peace, and it is harmony.

The 4 Dharma Seals

The 4 Dharma Seals are the distinguishing characteristics that define Buddhism. If particular teaching holds the 4 Dharma Seals, it is thought to be a Buddha Dharma. It does not matter whether or not you consider a particular belief or philosophy to be Buddhist; if the 4 seals fit within the philosophy, it is considered to be a part of the Buddhist path. The 4 Dharma Seals keep the purpose of Buddhism defined; without them, Buddhism would likely become just another religion. In Buddhism, there is no formal religion – it simply is what it is. You can follow the path of the Buddha through the teachings of almost anyone, as long as their teachings fulfill the 4 seals. The 4 Dharma Seals are: all compounded things are impermanent; all emotions are painful; all phenomena are empty, and Nirvana is true peace beyond description.

All compounded things are impermanent is the first seal. Buddhists understand this seal to mean that anything that is made of more than one part, anything that is assembled together, will eventually come apart. Since everything is made of more than one part, everything is impermanent. Remember:

change is inevitable. For instance, your body is not permanent. Every day from the day you are born, your body is changing. It is growing, maturing, and it is aging. Eventually, your body will cease to function — you will die. No matter how healthy you eat, or how much you exercise, your body will only exist for a little while. No matter how much plastic surgery you get, your body will still get older. Buddhists understand this concept; they accept it. The average person — not so much.

The importance of this seal in Buddhism is because it ensures acceptance of the impermanent. When you fully understand that nothing lasts forever, you can face each day with joy and peace. Why? Because nothing lasts forever. This means that even sadness and suffering never lasts. What is today may not be tomorrow. Accepting that nothing is permanent teaches you how to deal with the end of something when it comes. It can be a loved one's life or your career or something as simple as your favorite song — there is always a beginning, there is always a middle, and there is always an end. To accept this seal is to know this truth.

All emotions are painful is the second seal. This seal focuses on emotional feelings. Even feelings of joy and happiness have some sort of pain linked to them. How is this possible? Because nothing lasts forever. Everything changes, even feelings. Sure, you may be happy right now, feeling content and peaceful — but will you feel the same tomorrow? What if something happens that destroys your peace? All emotions are linked to pain. Your mind is dualistic — for every hope, there is a fear. Your emotions are tied to all aspects of your life. So, when you feel sadness, if that sadness is relieved, even just a tiny bit, you mistake that for happiness.

Your emotions are not independent. You do not feel a certain way without a reason. So, every action, every force that factors into your life, it all affects your emotions. All emotions are painful – they may not begin as pain, but the pain is there, just beneath the surface, waiting to rise to the top. Just as every good feeling has pain, every painful feeling has joy. Remember that nothing lasts forever, not even emotions. Buddhists understand this, and they know that only by releasing the hold that emotions have over them can they truly obtain a pure and peaceful mind.

All phenomena are empty is the third seal. In Buddhism, phenomenon are all things with characteristics. This seal teaches us that nothing is the way they appear. Think of a mirage – you see it, you believe that it is what it is, a phenomenon, an object right in front of you. However, the closer you get, the further away it gets. You are never able to reach it because it is not real. The emptiness that Buddhism speaks of is not a negative thing; it is just a truth that you must face. Things are not what they seem – they are empty of their supposed existence. Everything is comprised of emptiness.

This particular seal is probably the most difficult to grasp and understand. Some Buddhists pretend to understand the third seal. This mistaken understanding often leads to inappropriate behaviors for the Buddhist because he believes that everything is nothing, so there are no true consequences. This is not what the third seal means – it is an understanding that everything is empty, and nothing is at it seems. So, you do not have to believe in anything because there is nothing to believe in. Your only goal is to follow the path to Nirvana. With enlightenment, you will finally have a full understanding.

Nirvana is true peace beyond description is the fourth seal. Nirvana is not something tangible. It is not something that you can touch or hold onto or even see. It is beyond description. When you take away everything in your life that is fake, everything that gets in the way of your light, of your truth, you reach Nirvana. So, it is not a state of mind where you have everything you want – it is a state of mind where you have nothing, except true peace. You are enlightened.

The 4 Dharma Seals are the foundation of Buddhism. With a complete understanding and acceptance of these 4 seals, you will face life each day without fear, worry, or anxiety. You will know that everything changes, that nothing is what it seems, and Nirvana is a state of mind that you can achieve.

Chapter 5:
Buddhism Numbers 5

Moving right along into the next set of Buddhist teachings and the associated number brings us to the number 5. The following chapter will talk about two particular sets of 5 that are essential parts of Buddhism. As with the other information in this book, this is just an overview – it is your introduction to the world of Buddhism. With this information, along with other information you may have gleaned from a different source, you can make an informed decision. Buddhism is not necessarily for everyone, so you must arm yourself with the knowledge to determine if it is right for you.

The 5 Precepts

The first set of 5 we will discuss are 5 Precepts. You can think of these precepts as behavior rules. Together, they create a specific system of morality for Buddhists to follow. The 5 Precepts are a code of ethics, in a way, because they contain the basic "rules" you must adhere to if you want to follow the path of the Buddha. Your moral conduct, how you behave alone and around others, says a lot about the kind of person you are. As a Buddhist, your behavior must reflect the beliefs of Buddhism. There are hundreds of specific precepts in Buddhism, but the following 5 major precepts are the ones that are absolutely essential to the core of Buddhism. The 5 precepts are: abstaining from taking a life, abstaining from stealing, abstaining from sexual misconduct/misbehaviors, abstaining from lying, and abstaining from getting intoxicated.

- **Taking a life** – In Buddhism, to take a life, you are murdering any living being. It also includes the will or desire that you have to take a life. The more effort it takes to take a life, the worse the offense. For example, in Buddhism, it is worse to kill a big animal than a small one. While both go against the precepts, it takes more effort to kill a big animal, so that makes it a worse offense. When it comes to taking the life of a human, that, too, is always wrong. However, as far as how bad the offense is viewed under Buddhist beliefs, this depends on several factors, including the virtuosity of the victim – the more virtuous the victim, the more offensive the crime. Other factors involved in the level of offensiveness include the being, the perception of the being, the thought about the killing, the action of the killing, and the resulting death. There are also 6 ways that the taking of a life is carried out: by your own hands, through instigation, with missiles, by poisoning, through sorcery/magic, and through psychic powers.

- **Stealing** – This precept is straightforward. You cannot take anything that is not given to you. Therefore, you cannot steal anything. If you take what is not given to you, then you have the will inside of you to steal. The level of blame depends on different factors, just as with taking a life. The value of the stolen property is considered, as is the worthiness of the owner of the stolen property. Other factors involved in the level of blame include another being's property, being aware that the property does not belong to you, thinking of stealing, actually stealing, and the resulting completed theft.

- **Sexual misconduct/misbehaviors** — This particular precept pertains to your sexual behavior. It is quite specific in its code of conduct. This precept emphasizes the will to misbehave with someone "whom one should not go into," and actually carrying out the transgression through illegal physical contact. Here is where Buddhism might get difficult for some people. A person whom you should not go into refers, first and foremost, to men. Hence, it is safe to say that true Buddhism is not a supporter of homosexuality. There are also 20 different women whom you cannot go into. 10 women fall under a category of protection, such as by their father or another family member, or by their religion. The rest of the women include prostitutes, kept women, women bought with gifts, slave girls, female prisoners of war, and temporary wives. As with the other precepts, the level of offensiveness depends on different factors, including the virtuosity of the person you transgress with. There are four contributing factors for this offense: a person who should not be gone into, the idea of physically connecting with said person, the actions that lead to the offense, and the actual offense of sexual misconduct. The only way you can commit this offense is with your body.

- **Lying** – This precept refers to giving a false speech. You know that something that is false is not true. A speech is given under the impression that it speaks the truth. False speech is deliberately trying to convince someone that what you speak is the truth when you know that it is untrue. The level of offensiveness depends on the circumstances surrounding the act of the offense. For instance, someone asks you for a cup of sugar, but you only have enough left for yourself, so you lie and say you do not have any sugar. This would be a small offense under Buddhism beliefs and precepts. It is when you lie to convince others that you have seen something that you have not seen – that is serious under Buddhist beliefs and precepts. The factors involved are something that is not true, the idea of lying, making the effort to lie, the action of lying to someone else.

- **Intoxication** – This Buddhist precept is pretty simple. You have to avoid any intoxicants because they will cloud your mind, and they could cause you to act without thought and awareness. So, you cannot put drugs or alcohol into your body. Not only will this ensure that you always have a sharp, clear mind, ready at a moment's notice to meditate to a higher level, it also ensures that your body is purified of the intoxicants. As a Buddhist, you always need your mind to be pure and clear, so that you can follow the path to enlightenment without getting off course.

The 5 Skandhas

The Buddha listed the 5 Skandhas, also called the 5 Aggregates, as a way of understanding the different components that comprise an individual. The different pieces of the 5 Skandhas work together to create your sense of "I," your sense of a single self. In Buddhism, there is no "self," and there is no "I." The 5 Skandhas help you to better understand the concept that the "self" is just an illusion. The 5 Skandhas are as follows: form, sensation, perception, mental formation, and consciousness.

- **Form** – This skandha refers to form or matter, that which is material and can be sensed. The form includes 4 elements (fluidity, solidity, motion, and heat) and their corresponding faculties and senses (eyes for seeing, nose for smelling, mouth for tasting, etc.) Form is something that stands in the way of using your senses. For example, if a building blocks your view of the sunset, it has a form. If the sound of a train prevents you from hearing your music, the train and its sound has form. The same is true for anything in the way of your senses.

- **Sensation** – This skandha refers to the mental or physical sensation that you experience when your faculties (eyes, ears, nose, etc.) come into contact with the world around you. For Buddhism, you must remember that the mind is considered to be a faculty, the same as your nose or your eyes. The sensation is the experience of pain or pleasure associated with your senses.

- **Perception** – This skandha refers to how you perceive what is around you, whether it be forms or sensations. Perception is thought; it is your ability to think and to recognize things in front of you because of other related experiences. For example, you know that a shirt is a shirt, not because you came into this world knowing what a shirt is, but because you had experiences with shirts over your lifetime. You came to understand and recognize that a shirt is a shirt, a covering for the body.

- **Mental formation** – This skandhas refer to all volitional actions, no matter if they are good or bad. The mind is the leader of all mental states. If you have an impure mind, suffering will soon catch up to you. If you have a pure mind, happiness is yours to keep. Mental formation goes hand-in-hand with karma, which we will discuss in-depth later.

- **Consciousness** – This skandha refers to, essentially, a "cause and effect" through your faculties and senses. The particular faculty is the basis of consciousness, and it has a corresponding object. For example, your eyes are the basis, and seeing is the object. Your mind is the basis, and thinking is the object. Consciousness is awareness of the basis and object going together.

So, you may be wondering what all of this has to do with Buddhism, or you may be struggling to understand the concept of no "self" through these skandhas. The Buddha utilized the 5 Skandhas to demonstrate that each one is not "you," per say, but it is a temporary phenomenon. There is no permanence; they are empty. You cannot cling to these skandhas because you believe that they are what makes you, you – you must let go of these skandhas, and understand that they are temporary. They are not you. There is no self. There is only enlightenment and Nirvana.

Chapter 6:
Perfections of Buddhism

If you are going to practice Buddhism, you need to familiarize yourself with perfections. Without practicing the perfections, along with the other "rules", for lack of a better word, you cannot call yourself a true Buddhist. You will also never achieve the enlightenment you seek. Perfections are virtues that you can incorporate into your everyday life. By practicing the perfections, you will stay on the path to enlightenment. They are called perfections because you must practice them each and every day to perfection – you cannot stray from these guiding qualities. The perfections are a description of a true, enlightened being – the Buddha – and that is your goal, to reach the same level as the Buddha. Since there are different paths of Buddhism, we are going to look at two sets of perfections for two paths – the 6 Perfections of Mahayana Buddhism and the 10 Perfections of Theravada Buddhism.

The 6 Perfections of Mahayana Buddhism

In the Mahayana path of Buddhism, it is said that the Buddha spoke of 6 training bases for total and complete enlightenment. These training bases became known as the 6 Perfections. The 6 Perfections are as follows: Generosity, Morality, Patience, Energy, Meditation, and Wisdom. A closer look at each perfection will help you understand its particular importance in the path to Nirvana. It is important to note that all of the perfections work in conjunction with each; they support each other as a whole unit. However, there is a significance to the given order of the 6 Perfections. The first three perfections are virtuous, while the last three are spiritual.

1. **The perfection of Generosity** – Generosity is believed to be the gateway to the dharma. Think of it as your very first step in Buddhism. Generosity in Buddhism is not as simple as being generous in your life right now. Sure, you might donate to a charity once in a while, but what are you intentions behind that donation? A tax deduction? Bragging rights? Generosity in Buddhism is giving to others without expecting anything in return. It is selfless and pure. You want no recognition – in fact, you shy away from it. You want only to give to others because it is the right thing to do, not because it makes you feel proud. You give to others because it makes you feel good to help people, to bring joy and compassion into their lives.

The perfection of generosity can be divided even further than just general giving and helping. Generosity is divided into four categories: giving of property, giving of Dharma, giving of refuge, and giving of active love. Let us take a closer look at each category so that you will have a full understanding of generosity.

The giving of property is more than just giving someone food or shelter or clothes to wear. Your property includes every part of your body, so your organs, your eyes, your skin, and your life all fall under the category of property. It is important not to focus on whatever property you give away. Instead, focus on the action of giving without expecting or wanting anything in return. Even if you have nothing to give, you can still give with your state of mind. You can give your ears to someone who needs a friend to talk to. You can give your friendship to someone who is lonely. You can give comfort to someone who is hurting. There are many things that belong to you that you can give to others. Yes, it is going to be hard at first, especially when it comes to giving away your own belongings. However, keep your focus on the act of giving. Pay attention to the joy your giving brings to another. Over time, your will to give will only grow stronger.

The giving of Dharma refers to giving your teachings to others. Yes, personal items and material things are often needed and much appreciated. However, nothing lasts forever, so by giving the Dharma, by sharing and spreading all that you have learned in your journey, you are giving a gift that will keep right on giving back. You are teaching others to see the world through the right eye, to understand it, and to live their best life.

The giving of refuge refers to saving and protecting all lives of all living creatures. If you are actively participating in marches and meetings to bring an end to a war, then you are giving refuge.

If you rescue a small animal from a trap in the woods, then you are giving refuge. All life is precious, and all life must be protected. If a life is in danger, any life, then you, as a Buddhist, have a responsibility to help.

The giving of active love refers to wishing happiness and joy to all creatures. You want to spread the love, spread the joy, everywhere that you go. Sure, you can wish someone a joyful day, and their day might not be joyful at all. But if you wish them a joyful day every single day, perhaps they will start noticing the joy in their lives more often – all because you put the seed of joy in their minds.

2. **Perfection of Morality** – Morality in Buddhism does not mean blindly following rules, lists, and sets. All of those lists are guiding tools that you should use to achieve your own path to Nirvana. No two paths are ever the same. When you are enlightened, you will know how to react to any situation without having to remind yourself of any lists. Morality is the Buddhist way of developing compassion. There are three categories of morality: the protection of body, speech, and mind from unskillful deeds, protecting others as we protect ourselves, and performing skillful deeds protects us from unskillful deeds.

The protection of body, speech, and mind from unskillful deeds refers to making sure that you do not perform any unskillful deeds. You have to stop using your body, speech and mind in any sort of harmful way. You have to protect these things because if you do not, if you allow your body to act freely, your speech to flow without regard, and your mind to think without awareness, you are only setting yourself up for suffering.

Protecting others as we protect ourselves means preventing others from performing unskillful deeds. You have to stop someone from doing something wrong, such as hurting a living creature. By doing this, by stopping them from completing their cruel deed, you are protecting them from committing harmful deeds. You are giving them the same protection that you give yourself by helping them learn to control their own mind, body, and speech.

Performing skillful deeds ensures that we are protected from performing unskillful deeds is self-explanatory. By doing only skillful deeds, you are not able to perform unskillful deeds. How can you do something unskillful when all of your time is taken up by skillful deeds?

3. **Perfection of Patience** – Patience in Buddhism means being patient, tolerant, and enduring. You are able to withstand so much more than you even know. There are three categories of patience: patience when someone harms you, patience when you are suffering, and patience of keeping concentration.

The patience when someone harms you simply means not getting angry with someone when they physically or mentally bring harm to you. It also means that you cannot seek revenge on the person by trying to harm them back. Think of this patience as a coat of armor that protects you always from harm.

The patience when you are suffering means learning to accept responsibility for our own suffering. As a Buddhist, you believe in karma and rebirth; therefore, you know that any suffering you are experiencing is no one's fault, but your own. Maybe it was a week ago; maybe it was 125 years ago; but at some point, you planted the suffering seed, and karma has brought it back to you. You must have patience to cope with your own suffering. You must understand that everything is still as it should be – whatever suffering you are experiencing had to happen, the wheel of this suffering was set into motion as soon as you completed the action that planted the suffering seed. You can gain this patience by dealing with small sufferings at first, taking responsibility for them, and not blaming others. As your patience grows, you will be able to handle much bigger sufferings.

The patience of keeping concentration means learning to stay focused in your Buddhist studies, your meditation, and the spreading of the Buddha's teachings. You need patience to avoid any distraction from the Buddhism task at hand.

4. **Perfection of Energy** – Energy is in reference to being courageous in your path to enlightenment. You must develop and nurture your character, you must have spiritual training, and you must dedicate yourself fearlessly to helping others around you. You approach all aspects of Buddhism with energy,

with courage, and with integrity. There are three kinds of energy in this perfection: the energy of the mind that halts desire for regular things, the energy that shields us from growing tired and weary in our pursuit of Nirvana, and the energy of confidence in ourselves to attain enlightenment.

The energy of the mind keeps you focused on the dharma. Your love of normal things in life should never be greater than your love of the dharma. You actively pursue the dharma at all times of your life. You do not lay in bed for hours, thinking of nothing – you get up early, and continue on the path to Nirvana. You never waste any time in your pursuit of enlightenment.

The energy that shields us from growing tired and weary refers to always having the strength and ability to pursue enlightenment. This energy stops you from growing tired in life, tired to the point that you miss meditation, tired to the point that you stray from your path to Nirvana.

The energy of confidence refers to your ability to know and understand that you can achieve Nirvana, you can attain enlightenment. You are never too small or too weak to reach your Nirvana.

5. **Perfection of Meditation** – Meditation refers to intense concentration that nurtures your mind and brings you awareness and clarity. You must be able to calm and still your mind, as mentioned earlier when talking about knowing your own mind. You should be able to clear your mind, and practice mindfulness meditation without distraction from

your own mind. Meditation takes time to learn — you must practice, practice, practice.

6. **Perfection of Wisdom** — Wisdom is the realization and understanding of emptiness, that all things are without a "self," that all things are empty. This is an unequalled type of wisdom because it is the truth of Buddhism. Through the practice of the other perfections, you will attain this wisdom. Understanding emptiness in all things will help you to rid yourself of ignorance.

There you have it — the 6 Perfections of Mahayana Buddhism. Through these perfections, you can follow the path to enlightenment of Mahayana Buddhism. Each perfection has a purpose, and each perfection leads into the next perfection. By following the list and working on the development of each perfection, you will naturally segue into the following perfection on the list.

Next, we shall discuss the perfections associated with a different Buddhist path to Nirvana — the path of Theravada.

The 10 Perfections of Theravada Buddhism

As with the perfections of Mahayana Buddhism, the following 10 Perfections of Theravada Buddhism are listed in a very specific order. Each quality leads directly into the next quality on the list. One of the good things about perfections, whether you are on the Mahayana or Theravada path, is that you can nurture and grow each perfection in your everyday life. You do not have to be in a special situation to practice perfections. You just have to be conscious of the perfection you are working on. The following are the 10 Perfections of Theravada Buddhism, so you can see a few differences in the two paths to enlightenment.

1. **Perfection of Giving** – This is the same perfection as generosity on the Mahayana path. You are giving just to give, without seeking anything in return. You do not want to be recognized or praised for giving. You are giving because it is the right thing to do. When you give without expecting anything in return, you learn how to stop clinging to greed. You learn how to avoid becoming attached to things because, as you know, nothing is permanent.

2. **Perfection of Morality** – Again, this is the same morality discussed on the Mahayana path. You do not blindly follow the "rules" of Buddhism because the precepts and seals and even these perfections are guiding tools. They are meant to help you gain enlightenment your way because your personal path is unlike the path of anyone else.

3. **Perfection of Renunciation** – This perfection is not on the Mahayana path. Renunciation is the act of letting go. You let go of anything that holds you hostage to suffering and ignorance. It is letting go of the clinging, the clinging to all of the familiar things you hold dear. Nothing last forever, so you must stop clinging. You have to let go to be liberated.

4. **Perfection of Discerning Wisdom** – This perfection is the same as the other path. You seek the wisdom to know that all things are empty, to know that nothing is permanent.

5. **Perfection of Energy** – Again, this is the same perfection found on the other path. This energy ensures that you are courageous and fearless in your pursuit of enlightenment. Nothing gets in your way of following the path, not weariness, not fear, and not lack of concentration.

6. **Perfection of Patience** – As on the Mahayana path, patience has its own place on the Theravada path. The meaning of the perfection is the same. You are able to withstand much more than you ever thought you could withstand. You have patience when faced with someone intentionally harming you. You have patience when you experience your own suffering, and you take responsibility for your suffering. You have patience in concentration to ensure that you eventually reach mindfulness meditation.

7. **Perfection of Truthfulness** – This perfection is another perfection not listed on the other path. This perfection means you have no fear of speaking the truth to those around you, even people who do not want to hear the truth. It also means that you acknowledge the truth on your own. Truthfulness helps you stay honest and determined in your journey to Nirvana.

8. **Perfection of Determination** – This perfection is not on the other path, the Mahayana path. Being determined helps you understand fully what

you must do to achieve enlightenment. You are determined to reach your goal, and nothing will stand in your way. No matter the obstacle, you will approach it with a Buddhist mind, address it, resolve it, and stay on your path to the awakening.

9. **Perfection of Loving Kindness** – Here is another perfection unique to the Theravada path. With this perfection, you want to completely abandon any selfishness you might have, so that you can understand the suffering others, and give them compassion because you know that if they are suffering, then you are suffering, too. No longer are you focused on your own suffering because you have let go of that clinging behavior. Instead, you put your attention and energy to relieving others of their suffering.

10. **Perfection of Equanimity** – The final perfection on the Theravada path is that of equanimity. You no longer have the influence of your own ego affecting your thoughts, feelings, and actions. You are able to look at everything through a wise eye, through a neutral perspective because you understand the true reality around you

Perfections can be better understood if you think of them as priorities. Just as you have priorities in your current life, such as your family or your job. These things are on the top of your list of things to cherish, to protect, to nurture, and to value. The same can be said of perfections. You must make these perfections a priority in your life. It does not matter which path you are on – Mahayana or Theravada – the perfections have to be your first priority.

If you put your focus on things like money or even your relationships, you ultimately have no control over those things. Your boss can fire you without warning at any time, throwing you into a financial hardship. Your marriage could end without you even knowing that there was a problem. A family member could turn his back on you because he heard gossip about you that is not even true. Do you see how these things are beyond your control? However, with the perfections, they are within your control. You can always develop each perfection; you can always work on being a better person because of the perfections. This is within your control.

Chapter 7:
Mindfulness Meditation

One of the most important aspects of Buddhism is mindfulness meditation. This type of meditation is not your typical meditating session with soothing music playing in the background as you try to find your "center." That sort of meditation is found in various religions and practices – think yoga. Mindfulness meditation is much deeper than finding your center and calming yourself. This is a meditation practice that has a definitive role in Buddhism. Without mindfulness, you cannot practice true Buddhism. To understand mindfulness meditation, you must understand the meaning of mindfulness in Buddhism. Mindfulness is training your mind to be aware of what is happening around you, but without judgment or interference. While this may not sound exactly like a Buddhist belief, mindfulness is absolutely essential on the path to enlightenment.

You see, you can practice mindfulness in meditation within any religion or even just as an individual. Mindfulness is not an exclusive Buddhist belief. You can have a mindfulness meditation session with a group of yoga friends; you can have a session in the privacy of your home. There are no rules dictating who can and cannot use mindfulness meditation – it is a tool to reach higher levels of clarity, peace, and serenity. Many people from different religions, philosophies, and those just looking for a way to calm their minds have found mindfulness meditation one of the best meditation methods.

However, as mentioned before, you cannot practice Buddhism without mindfulness; therefore, mindfulness is a specialty of Buddhism. True Buddhists are experts at mindfulness meditation. They have reached a level of understanding and commitment to Buddhism that has allowed them to embrace the truths before them. They can participate in mindfulness meditation without any struggle; in fact, it is certain to be a part of their everyday lives. They can also help teach other Buddhists how to attain this most supreme level of meditating.

To practice mindfulness meditation, you must first understand mindfulness meditation. If you do not understand what you are going to practice, then you are only setting yourself up for failure. Even when you finally have a full understanding of mindfulness meditation, you will still have to learn how to bring it into your life. One does not simply dive into mindfulness meditation and succeed on their very first try. Here, we are going to discuss this type of meditation to ensure that you have a full understanding.

In the context of Buddhism, there are three major purposes to mindfulness meditation. The purposes are the reasons behind this form of meditation – they are your goals; they are what makes mindfulness meditation actually work. These three purposes – knowing the mind, training the mind, and freeing the mind – will take you down the path to the awakening. You must have a complete grasp of a purpose before you move on to understanding the next purpose. These purposes work together, and once you have achieved all three, you are well on your way to meditating mindfully.

Knowing the Mind

When you have a busy life, a full schedule, and little down-time, it becomes easy to get caught up in the everyday life without attempting to grasp a deeper understanding of your life. You need to know what motivates you, you need to be aware of your feelings and your reactions to every situation, and you need to have a clear understanding of the thoughts going through your mind. When you live life just going through the motions and trying to get through the day, your mind is not free, and it is not pure. It is distressed and tangled up in the chaos surrounding you. A chaotic mind will not find peace or clarity – not because it does not want to find peace and clarity, but because the chaotic mind simply cannot calm itself enough to find peace and clarity.

Knowing the mind helps you to pay attention to everything going on inside and outside of your mind and body. This means slowing down, bringing yourself to a mental and physical stillness, and taking time to get to know your mind. Even if you have a hectic mind, even if it is racing all the time, and you just cannot seem to slow it down, stop trying. Instead, focus on actually paying attention to each of those racing thoughts. Do not be critical of your chaotic mind – embrace it, and seek to understand it. The stillness that you need to achieve mindfulness meditation will only come with knowing your own mind. You must know your mind and body to achieve stillness, which is exactly what it sounds like – being still. Not just physically, although meditation of any sort requires that you sit still, but stilling and quieting your mind – bringing your mind to a standstill.

Back to the chaotic mind that is overflowing with thoughts and feelings. Each racing thought – grasp it, examine it, learn why it is there, and discover how it makes you feel, how it contributes to your overall happiness and well-being. When you make a conscious effort to understand your mind, when you take deliberate meditative steps to stilling your body, calming your mind, and learning why you feel a certain way about a certain thing, you are on the path to mindfulness meditation. It can take time to fully know your own mind. But once you do know your mind, you will find that you no longer feel compelled to change anything about it. You understand each thought, each feeling, and each reaction. You will be capable of observing your own mind from an unbiased perspective – and this is a very freeing experience.

To no longer have to battle your own thoughts, to no longer fight with your own mind to be quiet – it truly is the first step in mindfulness meditation. It is liberating because you are no longer bound by the chains of your overactive mind, your racing thoughts, your wide spectrum of emotions. Your mind is free to be still, to be quiet, and to let you be aware of the truths surrounding you. When you are no longer fighting your own mind because you finally understand it, you are free from the anxiety, worry, and stress that led to your chaotic mind in the first place. You are a quiet, peaceful observer who finally understands the reasons behind everything and every feeling – you are someone who knows their own mind, who is in touch with their own mind, and who is at peace with their own mind.

Training the Mind

After you know your own mind, you can begin to train your own mind. The mind is not just one thing that never changes. You are not born with the mind that you will die with. No, the mind is always changing. As we know through Buddhism, everything changes – nothing stays the same. This includes your mind. Think of it as a piece of clay. You are free to teach it whatever you want, free to shape it and mold it however you want. It is your mind, and it is right there, waiting for you to train it. When you come into this world, your mind really is a sponge – a description that is often attributed to toddlers. Your mind is absorbing and learning all of the time. Even as you get older, your mind is still learning every day. As the saying goes, "You learn something new every day." That is so true, especially of the Buddhist mind. A mind without discipline is a chaotic, overthinking, anxiety-filled mind – that is not a mind that is conducive to Buddhism.

The first part in training your mind is accepting responsibility for everything that goes on in your mind, for each thought and for each feeling. These are your thoughts and feelings. While we cannot control another person's actions, we can always control our reactions. So, if there is negativity, anger, hurt, or pain in your mind, it is your choice to feel that way – you are responsible for your own mind. If you do not take responsibility for your mind, you will not be the one shaping it. The outside world will shape it for you until it becomes a mind that no longer belongs to you – it is too affected by outside influences. You must embrace every thought and every feeling that goes through your mind as your own – after all, you put it there. You allowed yourself to think a certain thought or feel a particular feeling. You are in charge of your mind, and you must never relinquish this discipline.

Taking responsibility for your mind never ends. You must always be conscious of your thoughts and feelings, so if you sense them getting out of control, you can consciously reel them back in. To train your mind, start off slow. Teach your mind about kindness. Teach your mind about compassion. These are positive feelings that you can easily spread around you. You have to train your mind to let go of the negativity. You have to give your mind permission to forgive yourself for negativity. No one is perfect – that is the path of enlightenment, to try and reach a level of perfection in thoughts, feelings, and actions. During your Buddhist journey, you are going to have to face some truths within yourself about yourself. Learn to forgive yourself for whatever past action or feeling you had or still have, and train your mind to be kinder and more compassionate – not just to those around you, but also to yourself.

Learning how to meditate, not to mention how to mindfully meditate, is a process. You will not just sit down one day, decide to meditate, and be a professional. You need to ease into full-blown mindfulness meditation by training your mind one aspect at a time. Whether it be stability, concentration, courage, generosity, or kindness, take the time to train your mind in each aspect with due diligence. You want to experience growth of each aspect to its fullest before you train your mind to another. Each aspect that you learn will lead you right into learning another aspect. As your knowledge and understanding grows, so does your mind – you are training it to follow the Buddhist path. As you grow and learn and train your mind, meditation will come easier and easier to you.

Freeing the Mind

Freeing the mind refers to learning to let go. You see, clinging affects each and every person. By clinging, we are talking about hanging onto certain feelings or thoughts – you just cannot seem to stop clinging to them. As long as you are clinging, your heart and mind are not at peace. You must be able to let go of all feelings and objects of importance, whether they be good or bad, in order to experience an awakening, a true understanding – an enlightenment. Some of the things you might find yourself clinging to and struggling to let go of could be pleasure, desire, opinions, judgments, and even material possessions. You cling to what you know, and as a blossoming Buddhist fresh on the path, you are likely to struggle with not clinging to all of these things that have comforted you, kept you company, and been a part of your life for so long. But to be a Buddhist, you have to stop clinging – you have to let go.

Letting go of clinging can be a difficult task for the new Buddhist. You have worked hard to get where you are in life, you have worked hard for all of your belongings. However, understanding that nothing stays the same, and everything always changes, can help you to let go of the clinging. Why cling to material possessions when you cannot take them with you to the next life? Why cling to anger and hatred when it only brings your own positive energy down? Nothing around you will stay the same, so why not just let it all go? Letting go of clinging is actually very liberating – and that is a goal of Buddhism, right? To be liberated. To be delivered from everything you thought you knew, everything you thought was real, and shown the actual truth around you. Let go of clinging because it does nothing for you except prevent you from reaching your Nirvana.

Buddhism teaches you to let go of these things, to stop the clinging, so you can experience a free heart. You want your heart and mind to be liberated, to be delivered from all of the worldly thoughts and feelings and emotions that are holding you back, that are causing you to suffer, even with the happiness. Remember that even the joyful feelings have a connection to suffering because everything changes, and nothing ever stays the same – nothing is permanent. It takes time to free your mind and your heart. It is not going to happen overnight. You should expect to let go of the clinging one step at a time, one feeling at a time, one object at a time. However, once your mind is free, and you are no longer clinging to anything or any feeling or any thought, you will see that your mind is pure, your heart is free, and you are on the path to enlightenment.

Mindfulness meditation is essential to Buddhism because it teaches us how to understand the reality around us, to be aware, and to understand that nothing is permanent. According to the Buddha, we experience suffering because we do not have a full understanding of the true nature of reality. There is not anything in particular that is wrong with you or anyone else – you just lack understanding; you lack enlightenment. That is what Buddhism tries to show you – how to reach Nirvana and be enlightened about the true nature of reality. Mindfulness meditation teaches you to live with a full awareness, to live mindfully, and to concentrate on everything you feel and think, so that you can actually see reality for what it is without any judgment – just awareness and acceptance.

Simple Mindfulness Meditation Technique

Mindfulness meditation is not a form of meditation that you can jump into and be an expert. It takes time to know, train, and free your mind, so that you can reach the level of mindfulness meditation. However, you are likely curious right now about this type of meditation. It sounds very liberating, right? And since liberation is a goal of Buddhism, it seems as if mindfulness meditation is something you should be practicing from the beginning, right? Well, the answer is actually no. You cannot practice mindfulness meditation in its entirety as a newbie Buddhist. As we said, it takes time, lots of time, to reach this level of meditation. However, you can practice basic, simple meditation to help prepare your mind for what is to come.

If you want to give mindfulness meditation a shot, here is an easy technique to try so that you can get a little taste of what this type of meditation is all about. Keep in mind that this is not the whole of mindfulness meditation. Rather, this is a starting point for meditation in general, a starting point that you can use to begin your understanding and practice of mindfulness meditation.

- Find a quiet, comfortable place for meditating. You do not want anything to cause distraction, so comfort is important. Otherwise, you will find your mind straying to your discomfort instead of stilling and calming. Your environment needs to be quiet because you do not want to be distracted by crying children, the sound of the television, or the ringing of your cellphone. You need a peaceful environment to achieve peace of mind.

- Hands should be palm-down on your thighs, and your back should be straight, but again, comfortable. Rest your gaze about six-feet in front of you in a slightly downward direction. You are not focusing on any particular object; rather, you are simply gazing as your mind settles down. If you focus on a particular object, your mind will stay focused on that object. It will not be able to free itself from that object. You need to keep your mind clear of thoughts, so do not focus on anything in your sight – just gaze.

- Focus on your breathing, in particular, the breaths that come out. Stay aware of your environment, but put the focus on breathing out. Feel the air come out of your mouth and nose. Be aware that it is evaporating into the air around you. To get even more focused, pay attention to both breathing in and breathing out. Concentrate only on the breathing, and nothing else. Take notice of the air as it streams into your nose and mouth, filling your lungs. Then, take notice of all of the details as you exhale.

- If you find your mind drifting away from your breathing, remind yourself that you are thinking, and go right back to focusing on your breathing. The purpose of this is to take a conscious note of each thought or feeling that distracts you from your focus, and to put yourself back on the meditative path of concentration. You can even say out loud the word "thinking" or "think" as a sort of jolt to your mind that you lost focus. Think of it as training your mind much like Pavlov trained his dogs – his dogs responded to the bell, and your mind responds to the specific word. It helps to keep your mind clear, to teach you how to keep your mind clear at just the mention of a word.

When you are finished with your meditation session, you should feel calmer and more at peace. Your mind should feel more open, and you will want to take these feelings of peace with you throughout your day. There is no set time that you need to meditate. Meditate for however long you need to keep your focus and to clear your mind. Only when you have reached that calming, peaceful feeling, can you then bring yourself slowing out of meditation. Try not to end your meditation abruptly. Instead, allow yourself to become more conscious of your environment. Let the world around you slowly come back into focus. Darting back into reality can be quite a letdown, especially after a particularly great meditation session. So, take your time in bringing your mind back up to speed.

Mindfulness meditation is a very important part of Buddhism. Without it, you cannot truly practice Buddhism for all it is worth. Meditation takes time and effort to learn, so do not feel discouraged if you struggle to stay focused at first – every minute of focus trains your mind to concentrate, so every meditation session will get easier. Keep your focus simple at first, such as with the exhalation of your breath. As you develop your meditation skills, you can focus on larger aspects of the process. Pretty soon, you will be able to meditate fully for an extended period of time.

Chapter 8:
Karma

Karma – it is a word that you have surely heard and even used a time or two in your life. Karma is everywhere. It is in memes that you find on Facebook. It is in quotes that you find through Google. You have probably heard that "karma is a bitch." In a way, this can be construed as true, except that karma is not "being" anything. Karma is not on a constant search to punish people who put negative energy into the world. Karma is not a being; it is not a tangible object. Karma just is.

The Law of Karma is the Buddhist belief that every action has a result, every cause has an effect. You may understand karma as "what goes around, comes back around." Or perhaps, "You get back whatever you put into the world." These are both true of karma. Karma ensures that everyone is culpable for their own actions and the resulting consequences. Karma is a governing law that holds each one of us responsible for our own actions. There is no escaping karma; if your actions justify a negative consequence, that negative consequence – karma – will find you. It does not matter if your actions were from yesterday or ten years ago. Karma works at its own pace, but justice will seek you out. The same holds true for positive consequences because karma is both positive and negative – it is a teacher of lessons. If you deserve a positive consequence, karma will find you, and karma will bestow the positivity on your life.

In Buddhism, karma is easy to understand. You reap what you sow – the seeds you plant are the fruits you will receive. For example, if you are behaving in a manner that is motivated by anger or greed, you have planted a suffering seed. That suffering seed will eventually bloom, and you will be left with suffering. If you plant seeds of kindness and happiness, then those seeds will bloom into joy and happiness in your life. Karma really is the thought process of "getting back exactly what you put into the world." Think of it as planting an apple tree. Once you plant that seed for an apple tree, you cannot change it. It is an apple seed, and no matter how much you might will it to change into a tomato plant, it will always be an apple seed, and it will always produce an apple tree.

The only way you can change it is to remove the apple seed, and replace it with a tomato seed. However, if the seed has taken root, then you are only causing more damage by trying to remove it. You might as well just leave the apple seed alone because it is already growing. This is karma. You plant the seeds of anger, hatred, greed, pain, and betrayal, and you will reap only suffering of the same in return. You cannot change the seed once it is planted. You can change the seed once you see the error of your ways – but karma is already on its way to see you. Your actions of negativity produce only negative results. However, if you plant the right seeds, seeds of love, compassion, kindness, awareness, and acceptance, then you will yield the same positive results as the seeds you planted. You will yield happiness, joy, and peace.

Karma and rebirth, which we will discuss in the next chapter, essentially go together. You see, karma is not just the consequences of your actions in this lifetime – it is also the consequences of your actions in past lives. The Buddha believed in rebirth; through his meditation, he came to know several of his past lives. So, when the you of yesteryear, the you of a past life, commits a particular action, there are going to be consequences. Karma does not always act right away, nor does it necessarily act within a particular lifetime. This belief of rebirth and karma working together is how Buddhism explains occurrences, such as being born into a rich family or born in the projects; being born healthy and happy or being born with a physical or mental disability. These sorts of things are, according to Buddhism, the direct result of karma, whether it be karma from your current life or karma from a past life. Your actions will always follow you – and karma does not forget.

You must keep in mind that karma is not punishing you or your children by bringing them into an impoverished family or having them be born with a disability. On that note, neither is karma trying to reward you for good behavior. You are not a child, and karma is not your parent. Instead, karma is providing you with a lesson, a lesson on how your actions always, always have a consequence – it is simply the law of the universe. So, do not think that you are being punished because you have always been poor. Rather, think about getting in touch with your past lives through meditation, and discover why karma has given you this particular effect. If you are going to practice Buddhism, you have to embrace all aspects of it, including karma and past lives.

One thing to remember about karma is that the Buddha, when speaking about karma, focused on the intention behind each action. According to the Buddha, the intention, the motivation, behind every action is what determines how karma will return the action to you. This is why you are responsible for every good and bad thing in your life, for all of the suffering, all of the pain, all of the joy, and all of the goodness. You planted the corresponding seeds at some point in your life – and if your intentions were not pure, karma had no choice but to return those impure actions back to you. When you accept responsibility for everything in your life, both good and bad, when you understand that karma is not an evil force working against you, but simply a universal law that governs everyone, then you can start to make changes to your own karma.

You must be aware of your actions, of your thoughts, and of your feelings at all times. You have to release them, you have to let go, and you have to recognize that nothing stays the same – change is inevitable. Once you are aware of karma and the role it plays in your life, you can actually regain control of your own karma. You now know that planting the wrong seeds yields the wrong fruit. So, you can go forward in life planting the right seeds, and you can reap all of the joy and happiness that comes with the right seeds. It is not that karma is rewarding you or punishing you –

karma is simply returning the corresponding result to your action. You cannot behave badly in this world and expect karma to turn the other cheek. You have to learn that for every cause, there is an effect – and not always a positive one. However, it goes without saying that karma is not just about negativity. For every positive action you put into the world, karma will bring that positivity back to you. It might take a while, but karma will give you the appropriate consequences for your actions.

Karma is more than just one level of cause and effect. Yes, you ultimately get back exactly what you put into the world. However, there are also immediate results from your actions, results that are felt the exact moment you complete the action, good or bad. As soon as you do something kind or compassionate, you have the immediate gratification of feeling love and kindness inside – you feel good for having done something for the right reasons. The same is true for those negative actions. When you have a moment of anger or hatred towards someone, you are going to immediately feel the effects of that negativity. It is going to bring a painful energy to your life. As the talented Will Smith said, "Hate in your heart will consume you, too." This is a great comparison for the immediate results you get from karma. If you allow yourself to put forth that hatred into the world, it will immediately come into your field of energy. It will consume you from the inside because you are unable to stop clinging to it.

Karma is also a factor in understanding your personality, as well as the personalities of those around you. In Buddhism, there is no "self," and there is no "I." However, each one of us is a changing pattern of elements, a pattern of elements that make us unique from each other. Through understanding karma, you have created a specific state of mind. When you are kind and generous, you get the instant gratification, and therefore, you will want to continue doing those things for the good feelings you have, for the positive energy around you, and for the pureness of your mind. When you are mean and judgmental, you have the immediate results of that negative energy. It is easy for those negative feelings to become a pattern in your life, and as you continue putting forth "bad energy," you will continue to receive it.

It is easy to see the aspect of training your mind when talking about karma and personalities. You train your mind to feel a certain way, to think a certain thought. If you train your mind to be positive, it will be positive without hesitation. The same is true for teaching your mind to be negative. Pay attention to how you are training your mind. Karma, both the karma that has yet to come and the present karma, help you to train your mind. Training your mind to embrace the good and to release the bad helps to keep your current karma positive, as well as your future karma.

Your mind is a piece of clay – you choose how to mold it; you choose what thoughts and feelings are in your mind. You can choose to create a peaceful, loving mind, or you can choose to create a painful, suffering mind. Recognizing the negativity, being aware of it, and releasing it frees your mind to create new habits – habits of kindness and compassion.

Remember that your mind is a faculty, just like your eyes or your ears. You have to train it to feel and think the right things. Over time, as you are consciously aware of your thoughts and feelings, and you are keeping them positive, your mind will learn to respond on its own, without any urging from you, with positivity. Think of training as teaching your mind good habits. Over time and with enough practice, your mind will have the habit of being positive and joyful and kind and compassionate. Your mind will react accordingly because you have taught it good habits. If you dwell on the negativity, you will only teach your mind bad habits, ones that are linked to negativity, suffering, and clinging. You do not want karma to latch on to your negativity because it could mean years of suffering ahead. So, give karma something good to hang onto.

Again, karma is not here to punish or reward you. That would imply that karma is some sort of being, some sort of force that understands punishments and rewards. Karma is not a being or a force. It is simply a natural law that governs the universe. Karma does not differentiate between punishments and rewards. All karma knows is that for every action, there is a corresponding reaction – and karma ensures that the reaction takes place. There is no escaping karma – you will reap what you sow. That is why you absolutely have to take control of your actions. You must be aware, at all times, of the energy you are putting into the world, of the intentions behind every action you take. Karma already knows as the action is happening, so whatever happens is a direct result of something you did or did not do. So, go ahead and lend that helping hand to your neighbor. Embrace all people without judgement. Create a positive karma, both in the moment and in the future. Make the effort now to avoid putting anymore negativity into the world. If someone angers you, quell that anger through knowing, training, and freeing your mind. For if you recklessly put negativity into the world, you will never find your peace, you will never reach your Nirvana.

You must always keep your ultimate goal in mind when dealing with karma. The ultimate goal is, of course, Nirvana. It is enlightenment. It is the awakening. Karma will stand in your way of reaching your goal if you act in negativity. You need karma's help in going down the path to enlightenment. You need to put forth only positive energy – feelings and gestures of love, kindness, and compassion are a great place to start. Do these things not because you get a sense of pride from helping others – that pride is negative energy! Do these things because you are following the Buddha's path. You are a practicing Buddhist, and you love and cherish everyone around you. Keep your mind pure. Keep your thoughts joyful. Karma is all around you, monitoring your actions and the intentions behind each action. If you want to attain true enlightenment, then you have to live a life of positivity, so that karma will not get in your way later.

Understanding how karma, both future and present, affect your state of mind is an essential part of Buddhism. There are so many beliefs and practices and teachings that you must undergo to reach Nirvana. Keeping karma in mind at all times is only going to solidify everything you learn on your path.

Just as you can condition your body through exercise, and you can keep it fit and operating at its very best, so can you condition your mind. You do this conditioning through knowing, training, and freeing your mind. You teach it to respond in one particular way, so that you do not have to justify any negativity. You must have a pure and positive mind, a mind that knows its own thoughts and feelings, a mind that understands – that is the mind that will help you keep karma on your side. You just have to remember that karma is always watching. For every action that you perform, for every cause, there is an effect, both immediate and in the future. You choose what kind of fruits you reap from the seeds you plant. Karma only fulfills the choices that you make.

Chapter 9:
Rebirth

We have touched on so many beliefs, teachings, and practices of Buddhism. We have covered the origins of Buddhism and discussed the story of Siddhartha Gautama. We have reviewed a timeline of notable Buddhist events in history. You now have a better understanding of Dharma and the Eightfold Path. You know some of the more prominent "lists" or "sets" of numbers the Buddha created in his teachings – 3, 4, and 5 – as well as the perfections of both Mahayana and Theravada Buddhism. Mindfulness meditation was explained, hopefully in a way that you can understand, and you even have a simple meditation technique to try at home. You know how karma works, although you likely already had a good understanding of karma in the first place – you get back what you put into the world.

There is still much for you to learn about Buddhism. This book simply cannot cover every aspect of this way of life. However, it can provide you with the understanding you need of primary aspects of Buddhism, so that you will have the knowledge you need to decide if Buddhism is a philosophy you can apply to your life. Now, we shall discuss one last important teaching and belief of Buddhism – that of rebirth.

Rebirth is, to put it as simply as possible, the concept that your actions in life right now lead to whatever new existence you have in a future life after your current death. According to the Buddha, when he reached his awakening, when he reached Nirvana, he was shown his previous lives. He was also shown how living, dying, and being reborn have patterns, and that karma and rebirth are connected. This knowledge is crucial to Buddhism. Rebirth and karma have a definitive connection – each one affects the other. The Buddha understood this, and he sought to explain it to others, so that they could achieve the awakening that he at attained. When the Buddha was able to reach enlightenment, he was finally free – he would never be reborn again. The Buddha even taught his followers that once his current life was over, the world would never see him again.

Before we delve further into rebirth and its role in Buddhism, we have to address the elephant in the room – that elephant being the difference between reincarnation and rebirth. First and foremost, reincarnation is a belief belonging to Hinduism. Rebirth is a Buddhist belief. Rebirth and reincarnation are based upon the same general belief, which is that we do not have just one life. We have several lives during the course of our existence. There is no set number of lives that you might have during your existence. It could be only a few, or it could be hundreds. The difference between reincarnation and rebirth is how each person is introduced into their next life. You see, Hinduism stresses reincarnation, which is the belief that your soul is absolutely permanent. So, when you die in your current life, your body dies, but your soul moves right along into another body. You are born again into this world in a different body, but you are still the same person on the level of your soul.

In Buddhism, rebirth differs greatly from this belief of reincarnation. Remember, in Buddhism, nothing is permanent. Nothing stays the same, and change is inevitable. So, Buddhists do not believe in a soul transferring from one body from the next over multiple generations, but still being essentially the same person. That does not fall into the understanding that nothing is permanent. In Buddhism, there is no permanent soul – there is only a changing pattern of elements. This pattern of elements – this is you. There is no soul that stays the same throughout each of your numerous lives. Instead, Buddhism believes that your next life is determined by karma – your actions in your past life will determine your next life. The lives may be related in some way, but you are not the exact same person simply in another body. Your soul does not jump from body to body; rather, your actions jump from body to body. So, the actions of your past life, if they were negative, are going to force karma to put you in a life of equal energy. Your actions in all of your lives affect your next rebirth. It does not matter when an action occurred, karma is watching, and karma will give you the appropriate reactions. Your actions in life are what determine where you wind up in the next life.

The concept of rebirth compared to reincarnation can be difficult to understand. You just need to remember that reincarnation involves the soul, while rebirth keeps the focus on your actions, on how you live your life, to determine where your life begins next. Back to the story of the Buddha as related to rebirth, the Buddha determined that there were 4 stages to being awakened, to being enlightened. These 4 stages would determine how many rebirths you experienced over your many lifetimes. If you reach the first level of awakening, you will have as many as 7 rebirths. If you reach the second level of awakening, you will have only one rebirth back into the world of humans. If you reach the third level of awakening, you will have a rebirth followed by complete liberation. Once you reach the fourth level of awakening, you will not have another rebirth — your lives will end when your current life ends. This is why the Buddha said that the world would never see him again once his life was over — because he had reached the fourth level of awakening, and he knew that he would not be reborn.

You need to have a general understanding of these 4 stages of awakening, so that you are aware when you reach each level. These levels take time to achieve, of course, so you must not expect immediate jumps to the next level. However, knowing the stages will teach you how to recognize them when you reach them. Why do you need to recognize the levels? So that you will know where you are on the rebirth spectrum. Are you just starting, and you have many more rebirths to experience? Are you at the third level, so close to the fourth that you can barely contain yourself because you know that there will be no more rebirths? You need to know where you are when it comes to rebirth over the course of your existence. That way, you will not regress back to other ways of living, causing karma to disrupt your path to Nirvana.

In Buddhism, rebirth does not occur only on the human realm. You see, in Buddhism, there are many realms of the universe. These realms might be heavenly; they might be dismal. There are realms of animals, and even realms of ghosts. The human realm is just one of many realms that define the universe. So, in Buddhism, you could easily be reborn into an entirely different realm. You can also enter the human realm from a different realm – perhaps you were an animal in your most recent past life. This may seem like a hard pill to swallow, the idea of different realms. After all, this is not *The Lord of the Rings*. This is your actual life, and the idea that you might have been a cat in a past life can seem quite silly – almost as silly as worrying that you will be a ghost in your next life. However, if you are going to be a Buddhist, the idea and belief of these realms is something you will have to embrace.

Say it to yourself right now: "There are many realms to the universe. I am in the human realm right now. I may have come from a different realm in a past life. I may leave the human realm to enter a different realm when I am reborn." Saying it aloud can help make it more real for you, this understanding and believing in realms. Remember – the Buddha was an awakened and enlightened person. He was a real person who came up with all of these teachings. He was not randomly making things up – he wanted people to follow the path to Nirvana, so they could experience the same peace, joy, and understanding that the Buddha experienced. Ask yourself why he would ever have fabricated something like the different realms. He would not have fabricated anything, so if you believe the Buddha's teachings, then you believe in the realms. As astonishing and unbelievable as the realms might sound, you have to remember that it was not the Buddha's goal to deceive you – he only wanted to enlighten you.

Rebirth is probably one of the most difficult concepts for people to grasp and to accept. It is right up there with the realms. This holds especially true in the western world, where the idea of being reborn conflicts with traditional religions, as well as science. However, to be a true Buddhist, you have to embrace the concept of rebirth. There are Buddhist teachers out there right now that choose to teach Buddhism without rebirth. They teach Buddhism without rebirth because it has become so difficult for educated people to believe in rebirth. However, if you examine the history of Buddhism, you will find that it has always been hard to believe in rebirth. The Buddha faced plenty of skeptics with his teachings. However, he always stood behind his awakening – he never wavered in his belief of rebirth. While even a stripped-down version of Buddhism is likely to be helpful in some way, even if it is just learning kindness and compassion, it is not the Buddhism that the Buddha held true. True Buddhism, the Buddhism that the Buddha shared with everyone, so that they, too, could reach Nirvana – this is the Buddhism that the Buddha wanted you to learn, believe, and follow.

As mentioned in the previous chapter, karma and rebirth go hand-in-hand. For the Buddhist, there is a distinct connection between karma and rebirth. As mentioned, rebirth is believed to be based on your actions of a previous life – how you behaved, which seeds you sowed, determine where you are reborn. This is an important distinction to understand; it reinforces how important karma is to your life. Karma is really one of the key concepts behind Buddhism because karma has such a lasting effect on your life and your future lives. The actions that you complete in previous lives can affect your rebirth hundreds of years in the future. This is why you simply must live your best life every day, all of the time. Otherwise, you run the risk of being reborn into a negative effect from karma. Keep in mind that karma is not out to punish you or reward you. Karma is simply doing its job, which is ensuring that every cause has the right effect. Karma is always watching; it really cannot be said enough.

Rebirth is a difficult concept to grasp, as mentioned. People delving into Buddhism wonder if karma is real, if rebirth is real. With so many advances in science and technology, it has become quite difficult to grasp these beliefs that are believed based solely on faith. Even more traditional religions, ones that are easier to understand, have found many followers questioning beliefs. For instance, in Christianity, the Bible is like the teachings of the Buddha. Only it is the word of God and Jesus, and those words are the ones you must live by. The Bible teaches Creation, which is the belief that God created the world and all of its inhabitants in 7 days – 6 days if you do not count the last day, which was technically a day of rest.

However, with the advancement of science, there are many Christian followers who have found themselves questioning what they thought they believed. People of today understand science because it can be explained, it can be shown. To blindly follow a book of scriptures starts to go against the rational mind of some Christians. That is when they start the questions, and that is when their faith either holds up under the pressure, or it buckles, and they stop believing. Ideally, their faith is strong enough to withstand the doubting and the questions, and they continue to live their lives based on their religious beliefs.

Please bear in mind that this is not a criticism of Christianity. On the contrary, this is a superb example of how time and knowledge can change a person's faith. Knowledge can be a dangerous thing, especially when it comes to, essentially, blindly believing in something you cannot prove or see or even touch. The more that time has gone by and the more that people have gained knowledge, especially about science, the more likely it becomes for people to question their beliefs. It does not matter if it is Christianity or Buddhism that we are talking about – what matters is understanding that there are always questions when it comes to believing something purely on faith. That includes believing in the word of the Bible, and it includes believing in the teachings of the Buddha. There will always be someone asking questions, searching for rational answers, something she can see in a scientific manner to explain aspects of Buddhism. But when there is nothing to see, and there are only teachings to believe, it becomes a matter of faith.

And that is what rebirth is – a belief that is based on your faith in the words and teachings of the Buddha. No, he is not your God, and Buddhism is not exactly a religion, but more of a way of life. However, it might make it easier for you to understand if you put rebirth into that kind of context – it is a belief based on your faith, on what you believe in as a Buddhist. You have faith in the Buddha. You have faith in his teachings. So, even though you cannot see facts about rebirth or the realms or Nirvana on paper in front of you, your faith drives you to continue to believe, to continue the practices of Buddhism. Yes, rebirth does not necessarily fit into the "mold" of scientific teachings. There is no proof of rebirth, other than stories like that of the Buddha, and there is no proof that rebirth does not exist. When you reach a crossroads like this in your journey to enlightenment, you must ask yourself if you are truly ready to end your journey because you have doubts and questions. It is okay to have doubts and questions – your Buddhist teacher will help you find the answers. At the crossroads, do not choose the easy path of scientific, tangible facts. Take a chance. Take a leap of faith, and continue to pursue your very own Nirvana.

Some Buddhist teachers tell their students that it is not necessary to actually believe in rebirth as it is necessary to accept that it is a possibility. However, the Buddha made it clear that rebirth was a part of the path to Nirvana, right along with karma. The Buddha did not falter in his belief that karma and rebirth went together, that our actions in past lives determined our rebirth. So, it seems only fair to say that if you want to practice true Buddhism, then you have to do more than accept rebirth as a possibility, but you have to believe it based on your faith in the teachings of the Buddha. If you believe in the words of the Buddha, then you believe that eventually, on your path to enlightenment, you will be able to see and understand your past lives. However, just because the Buddha had his past lives revealed to him is no guarantee that you will have yours revealed to you. If rebirth is, in fact, a "real thing," you could live 17 lives without ever becoming aware of your past lives. So, again, believing in rebirth is a matter of faith, of believing the teachings of the Buddha, trusting in them, and living your life as such.

Speaking of karma and rebirth, their connection is important to Buddhism. Karma has such a huge impact on your current life, as well as your future life – even your future rebirths, should you choose to believe in rebirth. As a Buddhist, you must live your life with a full belief in karma; hence, it only makes sense that if you are believing in karma, then you are also believing in rebirth because of their strong connection to each other. It can all be quite overwhelming to think about as a beginner. The best thing for you to do is to continue learning about Buddhism through other books and through Buddhist teachers. This book is not going to give you all of the information you need to answer all of your questions about Buddhism. It is merely a starting point for you to give you a general understanding. Then, you can decide for yourself if you want to delve further into the teachings and beliefs of the Buddha – the philosophy of Buddhism.

Chapter 10:
Bringing Buddhism Into Your Everyday Life

As you have journeyed through this book, you have consumed a lot of information pertaining to Buddhism. You are likely a bit overwhelmed right now – there really is a lot to take in. In fact, this book only barely touches the top of all of the teachings of the Buddha. However, you are likely to have a general understanding of some of the most important aspects of Buddhism by now. The next question is to determine if you want to bring Buddhism into your life. If you want to learn more about Buddhism, there is plenty of information and resources available to teach you. If you have read this book and decided that you would like to give Buddhism a try, you must still continue learning. This book is merely a guide for a beginner. In no way does this book encompass all that is Buddhism.

With that said, as you start your journey down the path to enlightenment, you may wonder how you actually get started on bringing Buddhism into your daily life. No, you do not have to start wearing robes, and no, you do not have to join a monastery. There are no secret clubs to join, no Buddhist secrets to keep. The journey to enlightenment is just that – a journey. It has to start somewhere, so why not start with the first step? Here, in this final chapter, you will discover some easy ways that you can start to incorporate Buddhism into your everyday life.

Practicing Buddhism

The best way to start practicing Buddhism is to find a Buddhist center. Here, you will be given much more in-depth information about the teachings of the Buddha. These centers are made for beginners and established Buddhists. The atmosphere is going to be welcoming because, well, that is the way of the Buddhist – love, kindness, and compassion. There will be plenty of written information you can take home with you to study on your own. There will also be Buddhist teachers who will assist you in understanding all of the teachings. You will learn how to meditate, an essential aspect of Buddhism. The reason that it is always best to seek out a practiced Buddhist for teachings is because there is only so much information and understanding you can take from books and articles. Having a teacher to discuss your studies can be a great tool for traveling down your path to enlightenment with more ease.

As you begin your path to enlightenment, you need to learn all that you can about Buddhism. There are different paths to enlightenment, so you must study each one to find the path that fits your life the best. The different paths of Buddhism usually have the same basic ideas, but incorporate their own understandings of the Buddha's teachings into the path. So, you will find variances between the paths. There are thousands of books available to teach you about Buddhism. It is important to focus on one aspect at a time. If you try to cram in all of the Buddha's teachings as fast as you can, you are never going to understand what you are learning. You will also likely just get overwhelmed and fed up, leading you to give up on Buddhism.

A Buddhist teacher can help you with so many questions and aspects of Buddhism, so that you make the best choice for you. A teacher can also monitor your readings and studying, so that you stay focused without getting overwhelmed. However, not everyone has immediate access to a Buddhist center, so you may need to make the first steps on your own. Choose a specific aspect of Buddhism to study and learn. You want to absorb absolutely all of the knowledge of the aspect until you have a complete understanding. Only then should you move on to another aspect. Take your time with your studies. Utilize the internet to find other Buddhists online who will answer your questions and help guide you on your path.

You can start off slow, just simply learning some basic Buddhist terminology. You can start at the beginning, and delve deep into the story of the Buddha and the origins of Buddhism. The goal is to choose a place to start, stick with it until you really understand it, and then move on to another area of study. You can study as much or as little as you feel comfortable doing. Some people want to immerse themselves in Buddhism from the beginning – they are just that excited to go down the path of enlightenment. However, others choose to take a more cautious journey, taking their time with the teachings, asking all of the hard questions, and gaining as much insight as possible before taking even one more step. You decide how you want to learn about Buddhism – you are the only one who knows what is best for you.

Community is a crucial part of Buddhism. Buddhists need each other to learn from and to help guide. You need a strong, smart support system during your path to Nirvana. You cannot learn all that you need to learn alone. If there is not a Buddhist center near your location, then take to the internet. There are plenty of Buddhist forums, groups, websites, etc. that are full of practicing Buddhists who will provide you with the encouraging support system you need. They will also give you a place to take your questions, your anxieties, your concerns, and learn how to release all of them. Online groups can even help you with meditation.

One way you can bring Buddhism into your everyday life is to just take the time to sit every day. Sitting in peace and quiet is your first step towards mindful meditation. If you cannot sit still for a few minutes each day, completely still, then you have to keep practicing. Meditation requires a stillness of the body and the mind. So, start off with just sitting quietly. You do not necessarily have to worry about clearing your mind yet. You just want to ensure you can sit still for a bit of time. Start with five minutes each day. As you become more comfortable with just sitting in peace, add more time to each session. Eventually, you can start to bring meditation into the session.

Since Buddhism is a way of living your life, you have to be prepared to make many changes, especially in your awareness and understanding of the world around you and of your own mind. Awareness is a key point of Buddhism, so learning a proper meditation method is ideal. You must be able to clear your mind, to attain a level of purity in your mind that will lead you to enlightenment. You can practice meditation at home, on your own, with information you learn about meditation. You can practice meditation in a group setting with other blossoming Buddhists. You will likely find online groups where you can meditate "virtually" with a group. As long as you learn how to meditate, and you go further and further with each session into reaching that supreme level of a pure mind, then you are on the right track to enlightenment.

To bring Buddhism into your everyday life other than studying and meditation, just start living a kind and compassionate life. You want to put forth positive, happy energy in everything you do because, as you know, karma is watching. So, live your life knowing that karma will always find you. You are going to struggle during your Buddhism journey. There are going to be negative times as you learn more and more about the true nature of reality. You will likely have to face some hard truths about yourself and the way that you live or feel. Just keep going forward. You are not going to become a full-fledged, enlightened Buddhist in just a few weeks or months. You are looking at years of studying and practicing and changing and living your new life before you reach Nirvana.

While this probably sounds overwhelming, it will be worth the effort and the wait. Once you reach the level of enlightenment, you will no longer struggle with letting go of clinging, with accepting that all things change, with living a simple life, and with total awareness. You will be awakened – you will be like the Buddha. You will have a full understanding of your mind, your life, and your actions, as well as your feelings and thoughts. You will be a Buddhist, and your future will be very bright.

Conclusion

Thank you for making it through to the end of *Buddhism for Beginners*, let's hope it was informative and able to provide you with all of the tools you need to achieve your goals, whatever they may be. This book contained a lot of general information about Buddhism, from its origins to karma and rebirth. Take some time to digest this information. If your goal is simply to learn a little more about Buddhism as a potential belief system for your own life, then we hope that this book provided the insight that you needed to make your next step.

The next step would be, of course, to decide if Buddhism is a philosophical path that you want to follow. There is so much more to Buddhism than is contained in this book. The Buddha had thousands and thousands of pages of his teachings. Buddhism certainly is not an overnight philosophy. It is a way of life, and to embrace the teachings of the Buddha, you have to be willing to change your way of life.

Think of dieting – you can lose pounds over and over again with a diet, but if you do not change your lifestyle of eating and exercising, then you are destined to always gain the weight back, putting you right back where you started. The same can be said for Buddhism. You can pick and choose different Buddhist teachings to apply to your life, and you may experience more happiness and peace with the teachings. They may enhance your life in a positive way. However, if you do not embrace Buddhism as a whole, as a new way of living your life – a new lifestyle – then you will never reach Nirvana. You will never be enlightened.

Buddhism for Beginners is a great starting point for you to make your decision about bringing Buddhism into your life. Every journey begins with one step. Finally, if you found this book useful in any way, a review on Amazon is always appreciated!

Other Books by Judith Yandell

If you want to learn how to awaken and balance your chakras to bring joy and harmony in your life, then keep reading...

You might have a problem with your chakras without even realizing it. Do you experience headaches, neck pain or sore throat? Do you feel ill and emotionally unstable at times? Do you have troubles making decisions or feel lost and without a purpose in life?

These are just a few signs of unbalanced chakras.

If you experience any of these symptoms, I want you to know that there's a solution. You see, the 7 chakras are the energy centers of your body. If they're blocked or out of balance, you'll feel the repercussions in your body. If you want to reap the benefits of a healthier mind and bring harmony in your life, you have to balance your chakras and unlock their power.

Inside Chakras for Beginners, discover:
- How you can balance your chakras and heal your energy system to bring balance into your life
- What are the 7 chakras and how do they work
- The locations and functions of the 7 chakras, from Root to Crown
- 5 lessons for clearing chakra blockages and bringing harmony and balance in your life
- How damaged chakras are affecting your life and how you can heal them (many people don't even know they have chakra blockages)
- Lists of questions to help you concentrate on the specific energy of each chakra and balance each one more effectively.
- Why balancing chakras is important and why everyone should be doing it.
- Helpful techniques and practices to keep your chakras open
- Useful strategies to bring harmony and balance in your life.
- Kundalini techniques and practices to awaken your chakras
- The most common issues created by a clogged chakra system and how to solve them

- 7 effective meditations, one for each chakra, to help you clear energy blockages and enhance your life

And much, much more!

Even if you have zero knowledge about chakras and energetic balance, this beginner's guide will help you clear your whole chakra system and live your life in harmony and balance. The truth is, when you learn how to activate and clear your chakras, they will let positive energy flow to every part of your body, mind and spirit. So, if you want to heal your body and spirit and balance your chakras to bring joy and wellness into your life, grab your copy now.

"Chakras for Beginners" by Judith Yandell is available at Amazon.

We all feel some kind of empathy towards others. But if you have no control over your empathy and always have the obsession of fixing other people, then you know how painfully frustrating being an empath is.

Empaths are usually overwhelmed by other people's emotions, they feel what others feel and are able to profoundly understand their mind. As a result, empaths care for everyone else but themselves. They become "magnets" for negative people that want to take advantage of the empaths' ability to understand opinions and emotions of others.

However, I want you to know that being an empath doesn't have to be so negative. You may have not yet realized it, but you have a powerful and beautiful gift. If you learn how to embrace it and channel your empathy, you can use it for spreading kindness, love and positive energy to the world.

In this book you'll learn:
- 6 Powerful Methods You Can Use to Control Your Gift (Hint: They Don't Include "Avoid Social Situations" and "Lock Yourself Up in You House")
- The Single Most Effective Thing You Can Do to Shield Yourself From Energy Vampires
- 11 Most Common Personality Traits of Empaths
- Powerful Techniques to Develop Your Skills and Channel Your Empathy to Spread Positive Energy
- How To Use a Specific Kind of Negative Thinking to Actually Overcome Your Social Anxiety
- 20 Statements to Help You Determine if You Really Are an Empath
- Is an Energy Vampire Preying on You? Here's How to Find Out
- How to Find Out if Your Child Is an Empath and What You Can Do to Support
- A Positive Affirmations Routine That Can Help You Accept Yourself as an Empath and Strengthen Your Abilities
- How Detoxifying a Certain Area of Your Brain Can Help You Embrace Your Empathic Abilities and Improve Your Sense of Intuition
- Why in Certain Cases Accepting Negativity Can Actually Help You Feel Better.

Even if right now you feel you have no control over your abilities, I want you to know that you can learn how to manage your empathy and develop your gift in the right way.

**"Empath" by Judith Yandell
is available at Amazon.**

Made in the USA
Columbia, SC
12 February 2025